TECHNOLOGY

IN THE SECONDARY SCIENCE CLASSROOM

TECHNOLOGY

IN THE SECONDARY SCIENCE CLASSROOM

Edited by Randy L. Bell, Julie Gess-Newsome, and Julie Luft

Claire Reinburg, Director
Judy Cusick, Senior Editor
J. Andrew Cocke, Associate Editor
Betty Smith, Associate Editor
Robin Allan, Book Acquisitions Manager

Art and Design
Will Thomas, Jr., Director
Tracey Shipley, Cover and Interior Design

Printing and Production
Catherine Lorrain, Director

National Science Teachers Association
Gerald F. Wheeler, Executive Director
David Beacom, Publisher

10 09 08 4 3 2 1

Library of Congress Cataloging-in-Publication Data

Technology in the secondary science classroom / edited by Randy L. Bell, Julie Gess-Newsome, and Julie Luft.
p. cm.
Includes bibliographical references and index.
ISBN 978-1-933531-27-4
1. Science--Study and teaching (Secondary)--Data processing. 2. Educational technology--Study and teaching (Secondary) I. Bell, Randy L. II. Gess-Newsome, Julie. III. Luft, Julie.
Q183.9.T43 2008
607.1'2--dc22

2007040668

This book was made possible by NSF grant #0540041. The ideas expressed in this book are those of the authors and do not necessarily represent the view of personnel affiliated with the National Science Foundation.

CONTENTS

PREFACE

Technology in the Secondary Science Classroom, and its companion volumes, *Science as Inquiry in the Secondary Setting* (now available from NSTA), and *Science Education Reform in the Secondary Setting* (in development at NSTA), has a long and interesting history. The ideas for these books emerged from our work with secondary science teachers, supportive program officers at the National Science Foundation, and the science education community, which is always seeking a connection of theory and practice. In order to ensure that these books were connected to each of these stakeholders, we adopted a writing plan that involved representatives from all three groups. We considered novel approaches to identify and support science teachers and science educators to participate in the project, and we sought guidance from program officers about the format and dissemination of the final product.

To begin with, we identified three topics of interest to both science teachers and science educators. We wanted the community of science educators to help define the content of each book, so we solicited chapter proposals from science teachers and science educators. The response was impressive, with over 50 chapter proposals submitted for the three books. Our selection of the chapters was based upon the clarity of the topic, the type of idea presented, and the importance of the topic to science teachers.

Chapter authors were then asked to generate a first draft. These chapters were shared among the authors of their respective books for review. We met as a group at the annual meeting of the Association of Science Teacher Educators, in Portland, Oregon, to discuss and provide feedback to one another on our chapters. This session was extremely useful, and several of the authors returned to their chapters, ready for another revision.

Once the second revision was complete, we wanted to draw upon the expertise of science teachers, whom we felt should ground this work. We contacted the National Science Teachers Association (NSTA) and placed a "call for reviewers" in their weekly electronic newsletter. Over 200 teachers offered to review our chapters. Reviews were shared with the chapter authors.

The second revision was also shared among the authors within each book. Each author now had external reviews from teachers, as well as reviews from other authors.

To discuss these reviews and the final revision of the chapters, we met one more time at the annual meeting of the National Association for Research in Science Teaching, in San Francisco, CA. At the conclusion of this meeting, chapter authors were ready to write their final versions.

When the chapters were completed and the books were in a publishable format, we approached NSTA about publishing them both in print and online, so that they would reach as many teachers as possible. The editors at NSTA felt the time was right to attempt to offer the chapters of these books free online for teachers. NSTA has historically offered one chapter of a book for free, but the opportunity to break new ground by offering each chapter of this book free online would be new publishing territory. Of course, paper copies of each book are available for purchase, for those who prefer print versions. We also asked, and NSTA agreed, that any royalties from the books would go to NSTA's teacher scholarship fund to enable teachers to attend NSTA conferences.

This process has indeed been interesting, and we would like to formally thank the people who have been helpful in the development and dissemination of these books. We thank Carole Stearns for believing in this project; Mike Haney for his ongoing support; Patricia Morrell for helping to arrange meeting rooms for our chapter reviews; the 100+ teachers who wrote reviews on the chapters; Claire Reinburg, Judy Cusick, and Andrew Cocke of the National Science Teachers Association for their work on this book; Lynn Bell for her technical edits of all three books; and the staff at the National Science Teachers Association for agreeing to pilot this book in a downloadable format so it is free to any science teacher.

Julie Luft, Randy Bell, and Julie Gess-Newsome

Educational Technology in the Science Classroom

Glen Bull and Randy L. Bell

Technology has transformed the way in which science is conducted. Almost every aspect of scientific exploration has been touched in some way by technology, and much of today's science would not be possible without it. The mapping of the human genome, astronomical observation, weather forecasting, and the development of emerging nanotechnologies are all dependent upon information technology.

Information technology is simultaneously transforming society. The way in which leisure time is spent is very different than a few years ago. In the last half of the 20th century a typical child watched television an average of three to four hours per day. This experience essentially consisted of passively viewing materials created by others.

The most recent Pew Foundation survey (2005) found that 87% of all teenagers report using the internet. The majority of students interact with one another socially via the web. They use text messaging, voice over internet protocol (VOIP) communications, and videoconferencing to communicate with one another. They interact with and use online media—digital music, video, and news accessed through the web.

Students are also becoming content creators—creating and sharing media such as original artwork, digital photographs and videos, blogs, and web pages. Many of these students have grown up with the internet and can be characterized as digital natives.

The nation has made a concerted effort to provide the infrastructure that will make it possible to employ these technologies in school, as well. Each year billions of dollars are invested in establishing an effective infrastructure for employing information technology in schools. Almost all classrooms have been wired for internet access, computers have been installed, and inservice sessions are being offered to demonstrate ways in which technology can be employed. The ultimate goal is to enhance student learning.

Some science teachers have been in the forefront of this technological transition. These innovators and early adopters have integrated microcomputer-based probes into their laboratories, employ digital videos and imagery to illustrate concepts in class discussions, and are using administrative programs and electronic gradebooks to organize their classes.

Other teachers are waiting until best practices emerge that will allow them to determine the conditions under which gains in learning outcomes justify use of technology in the classroom. This book serves science teachers in both categories.

It has long been our philosophy that technology can be worth the time and expense when (a) it is used to address worthwhile science in ways that are pedagogically appropriate, (b) it makes scientific views more accessible, and (c) it helps students be able to engage in science learning they could not otherwise do without the technology (Flick and Bell 2000). A base of research literature is emerging that provides evidence that some computer tools are effective in these areas. Practically speaking, computer technologies that will appeal to the widest variety of science teachers should also be easy to learn and should, ideally, be able to address a wide range of science topics.

The goal of this book is to provide an overview of a range of computer technologies having the potential to help students better learn science content. Some of these technologies are relatively easy to master—the majority of American households now have a digital camera, for example, because they are inexpensive and easy to use. Other technologies such as some geographic information systems and digital probeware will appeal to those who welcome the challenge of more complex systems.

We hope that each chapter will stimulate your thinking about the potential of these tools to engage your students in science learning. The chapters that follow offer a snapshot of the latest trends, providing for each technology:

(1) A summary of current research regarding the technology's effectiveness and classroom implications
(2) Best practice guidelines for teaching with the technology, drawn from the research and practitioner literature
(3) A few innovative ideas for teaching science content with the technology tool

Pedagogy + Technology + Content

The chapters that follow provide insight into ways to employ technology both to address existing educational objectives and to examine possibilities for exploring new conceptual frontiers. The technology itself is typically neutral—it is only when a technology is combined with an appropriate teaching strategy that it becomes effective.

Therefore, the technology cannot be discussed in isolation—it must be combined with a description of the teaching strategy. A description of the manner in which a *pedagogical strategy* is combined with *technology* to teach specific *content* is crucial.

Pedagogy

The authors of the chapters that follow provide illustrations and examples of pedagogical strategies in a range of contexts. Often the same technology can be used for a variety of instructional approaches. For example, classroom use of a virtual planetarium is discussed in Chapter 3 on simulations. As this chapter indicates, virtual planetarium software can be used in a number of different ways—for direct instruction (e.g., to orient students and provide scaffolding) or in a student-centered, experiential way.

As illustrated in Table 1, either of these approaches could be employed in the computer lab or through whole class instruction with the aid of a computer projector.

Table 1. School uses of information technology.

	Classroom	Computer Lab
Direct Instruction	X	X
Student Inquiry	X	X

These approaches are not mutually exclusive. In some instances the teacher might choose to scaffold a computer activity through direct instruction in a whole-class setting followed by a student-centered inquiry-based experience.

Technology

Technology provides a means to good science instruction but is not an end in itself. To be effective, technology must provide tools that facilitate and enhance instruction. Improving data collection, visualization of abstract phenomena, and simulations of experiments that would otherwise be impossible in school classrooms are some specific ways that technology can enhance student engagement and learning.

In practice, every technology tool involves a certain amount of instructional overhead. The ideal technology has a low threshold and a high ceiling. In other words, it will be intuitive for the novice to learn and yet support increasingly sophisticated activities.

If the technology will be used for a wide range of topics through the entire school year, the time required for mastery may be a good investment. On the other hand, if a tool will only be employed for a lesson or two, the functions of the tool must be straightforward to justify its use.

Advances in technology and user interface design can make tools that were once cumbersome to use more accessible. For example, probeware at one time was difficult to install and configure. A newer generation of scientific probeware that interfaces directly with standard USB ports has simplified configuration and setup.

Content

People who enjoy new gadgets may be tempted to incorporate technology into the science classroom for its own sake. However, technology use is more appropriate when it enhances the learning of worthwhile science concepts and process skills. It should be used to help students explore topics in more depth and in more interactive ways and to promote student-centered, inquiry-based learning.

Many scientifically accepted ideas are difficult for students to understand due to their complexity and their abstract or counterintuitive nature. A number of studies have documented the potential of specific educational technologies to make scientific concepts more accessible through visualization, modeling, and multiple representations. Many of these studies are cited throughout the chapters of this monograph.

As a practical matter, educational technologies must support existing instructional objectives in order to be effective, and science activities should not be developed merely because technology makes them possible. An increasing emphasis has been placed on educational accountability in recent years. Instructional objectives identified at the state and national levels reflect the distillation of considerable effort by expert groups. Although technology can sometimes offer the opportunity to add new objectives to this inventory, it is most likely to be used when it can also address existing educational objectives as well—especially those found on high-stakes assessments.

A Framework for Integrating Technology

Much of the value of information technology can be found in its capability to allow students to work with data, to enhance visualization of complex concepts or of unfamiliar places and objects, and to facilitate communication and collaboration.

Data Collection and Analysis

The *National Science Education Standards* Science as Inquiry Standard (NRC 1996) stated that all students need to learn how to *analyze evidence and data* by, for example, determining the range of the data, the mean and mode values of the data, plotting the data, developing mathematical functions from the data, and looking for anomalous data. The Standards suggest that the data analyzed can be drawn from students' own investigations or from other students' investigations, but can also be acquired from external scientific databases. They also recommend that computers be used for collection, analysis, and display of data. The chapters that follow address use of technology in this manner.

Real-world data has an inherent messiness, with anomalies sometimes cropping up. It is productive to allow students to understand the nature of the scientific data collection process. This is the rationale for scientific laboratories. Technology simply extends these capabilities, just as it has for scientists themselves. Chapter 4 on scientific probes describes ways in which these tools can be used to support scientific inquiry. Similarly, Chapter 5 describes how specialized sensors in geosynchronous Earth satellites can be used to acquire data that can extend scientific exploration by students.

Much of today's science involves acquisition of massive databases by teams of scientists and others. These databases exceed the capabilities of a single student or class to replicate. Fortunately, in the spirit of scientific sharing, many of these databases are freely available on the web. Chapter 6 on acquisition of online data describes how these databases can be employed to facilitate scientific analysis and understanding.

Scientific simulations are derived from models based on data collected by scientists. These models can be useful in allowing students to visualize patterns that would be difficult to understand otherwise. Chapter 3 on scientific simulations describes research indicating that this approach can be effective in enhancing student learning.

By combining the triad of data collected by students, data collected by scientists, and scientific simulations and computer models derived from scientific data, science teaching can take advantage of new facilities for enhancing student learning. Technology can allow students to explore data, make predictions, and form conclusions. It can be used to confirm textbook assertions but is perhaps most powerful when it also facilitates inquiry and guided discovery.

Imagery and Visualization

The value of imagery for understanding scientific concepts is well known. Technology has improved access to science-related digital photographs and video. It has also improved the feasibility of students collecting their own visual data. Digital cameras are perhaps the most ubiquitous technology in society today. Digital cameras have been incorporated into cell phones and personal organizers. Thousands of webcams with live feeds now span the globe. Millions of publicly available images are being uploaded to photo-sharing services. The next generation may become the best documented visually.

Chapter 2 describes best practices for use of both still and moving images in the science classroom. Although images can be valuable for learning, the research available to date indicates that this only occurs under certain conditions. These conditions are described in the chapter, along with illustrations and suggestions for ways in which digital images and video can enhance learning.

Communication and Collaboration

The advent of the internet has changed the way in which scientists communicate and collaborate and it is changing science teaching as well. Chapter 7 describes ways in which the web can be used to support science inquiry in teaching. Often these projects take place in a conventional classroom but take advantage of the web to extend the boundaries of the project in ways that would not be practical otherwise. For example, the National Geographic Society Kids Network Acid Rain project allowed students across the United States to measure the acidity of local rainwater and aggregate these results to construct a composite picture around the world in concert with the efforts of similar classes. As noted in Chapter 7, it is the combination of the web-based tools and capabilities in concert with a specific inquiry-based teaching strategy that produces the outcomes associated with these kinds of initiatives.

Distance Education and Evaluation

The internet has also enabled distance education. Distance education is rapidly growing at all levels: in high schools, community colleges, and research universities. Theoretically, all the advantages of online technologies can be available through virtual science classes. Chapter 9 summarizes what is currently known about best practices associated with teaching and learning science in virtual science classrooms.

Computer technologies have affected other areas of education, as well. Many teachers have adopted administrative technologies to help them keep track of assignments and grades and computerized testing programs that provide banks of test questions. Since this book is about uses of technology to teach content, Chapter 8 describes an innovative use of online assessments to encourage student collaboration in their science learning.

Summary

At the dawn of the computer age, then-director of the U.S. Office of Scientific Research Vannevar Bush published an influential paper, "As We May Think" (1945). This paper attempted to consider the implications of a world in which all information would be stored with the capacity to create associative links between related materials. This visionary essay ultimately influenced innovators who conceived the computer mouse and the modern graphical interface as well as the subsequent development of the internet.

Today we are rapidly approaching an era in which the majority of the world's information is digitally stored and searchable. Schools have arguably been affected by technology less than any other aspect of society. In certain respects this is appropriate; schools are conservative institutions, so will be less subject to fads and shifting educational cycles. However, it is clear that the digital revolution is anything but temporary—it is a permanent change that is affecting all of society.

The question to consider is how this capability may be best employed, both in society and in science teaching. If you are an early adopter, you should find some interesting new concepts here for using computer technologies in your science classroom. On the other hand, you may have been waiting to be convinced that computers offer more to the science class than expensive bells and whistles. The chapters that follow describe many ways in which even inexpensive technologies combined with appropriate teaching strategies can be effective at helping science students learn science concepts more effectively.

Digital Images and Video for Teaching Science

Lynn Bell and John C. Park

With its emphasis on empirical evidence, a great deal of science and science teaching involves observation. Science teachers also know that students can better understand complex scientific concepts when they can see the phenomenon they are studying. That's why science textbooks are filled with photographs and diagrams, and science classrooms typically include microscopes, specimens, and models.

New technologies have revolutionized our ability to see and learn scientific phenomena. Reasonably priced digital still and video cameras have recently become popular additions to many classrooms, and teachers use them regularly to document student learning activities for newsletters, websites, and electronic slideshows. In addition, the advent of the internet has opened up a limitless supply of images and videos on every imaginable science topic.

This chapter will focus on how science teachers can take advantage of the digital images and video available to them on the web, as well as on how to engage students in capturing their own images and video in the process of learning science.

Digital Images in Science Learning

The idea of using pictures in a science classroom is not new. In the late 19th and early 20th centuries science educators advocated the use of drawings to help students learn science. With the invention of film cameras, science textbooks began including more and more photographs, and methods textbooks were written on how to use photographs, slides, filmstrips, and opaque projectors effectively in science teaching.

The quantity and availability of high-quality science-related photographs has exploded with the growth of the internet. Numerous reliable websites provide digital images specifically dedicated to educational use. These resources provide a convenient supply of ready-made images for observing, analyzing, inferring, and questioning.

If you are fortunate enough to have one or more digital cameras in your classroom, students can capture their own visual data and record their experimental results for further analysis. Digital cameras can record not only individual images—including those viewed through an attached microscope or telescope—but they can also record a series of images over time that can be converted to video to capture movement otherwise too slow to view.

Digital Video in Science Learning

Instructional movies also have a long history in schools. As far back as the 1930s, educators and researchers were examining the use of motion pictures to allow students to view events too fast for the unaided eye to catch or to enable students to view events they could not otherwise see because of time or location constraints. In the 1980s easy-to-use video cameras became available, allowing teachers and students to create their own movies for classroom use.

The combination of digital video technology, the web, and inexpensive digital video editing software has improved both the availability of instructional videos and the opportunities for students to create their own works, while also bringing a number of other advantages. Digital videotape or other solid-state media can be transferred to computers for playing or editing. Some cameras can even record digital video directly to the computer hard drive. Users have random-access ability to locate specific scenes on the video rather than having to watch in a sequential linear fashion or move through a length of film or tape to get to the desired location. Digital movies can also be slowed down and scenes can be advanced or reversed one frame at a time.

Software that enables basic video editing comes installed with newer computers (e.g., iMovie for Macs or Windows MovieMaker for PCs) or may be purchased for around $100. With this software, users can delete unwanted scenes from video or cut out short video clips from longer footage.

Very recently, a number of web-based video editors have become available. As they are further developed and refined, these web-based programs will offer two significant advantages for school-based projects: (a) Because both the software and the video product are stored online, students will be able to work on a project from any computer with internet access and (b) video files created online will be instantly available for sharing with other viewers (for more information see Working With Video On the Web, p. 11).

These flexible features all make using video more adaptable to educational needs than ever. In addition, access to good quality instructional videos has increased. Video can be easily shared on and retrieved from the web. There are even commercial companies with large libraries of instructional video content that can be streamed via the web to school classrooms (e.g., Discovery Education's *unitedstreaming*). Recently, the nonprofit organization Next Vista established a website (*www.nextvista.org*) that disseminates open educational digital media, including videos on science topics.

WORKING WITH VIDEO ON THE WEB

This is a rapidly changing area, but some of the first examples of web-based video editing software include:

- Jumpcut (*www.jumpcut.com*)
- Motion Box (*www.motionbox.com*)
- VideoEgg (*www.videoegg.com*)

These services typically permit a certain number of megabytes of video files to be posted at no charge, with modest fees for larger files.

Other sites are popping up that allow users to store short videos online at no charge. To find them, search on names like YouTube, Vimeo, vSocial, DailyMotion, and OurMedia.

Video tagging services are also appearing, which allow users to create tags linked to individual sections of video, so that viewers can skip straight to relevant sections. Some early tagging services include MotionBox, Click.TV, and VeoTag.

What the Research Says

Digital Images

Since the dawn of personal computers much visualization research has focused on modeling and animations, and there has been little to no research on using digital images in teaching and learning. In prior generations, however, a great deal of research was done on the role of pictures in learning (especially pictures paired with text, as in textbooks), and that research can be transferable to the topic of digital images today.

John Bransford and his colleagues (Bransford 1979; Bransford and Johnson 1972) conducted some of the more well-known studies on pictures and learning. They determined that a picture can increase comprehension and recall by providing context before students read a passage—a form of advance organizer.

Levie and Lentz (1982) reviewed 55 studies investigating how representational pictures affected learning of information presented in written texts. They concluded that these studies provided overwhelming evidence of a significant positive effect of pictures on learning related text information—both in terms of comprehension and recall.

A few years later, Levin summed up the essence of the research findings on the role of pictures in learning in this way: "Pictures interact with text to produce levels of comprehension and memory that can exceed what is produced from text alone" (1989, p. 89).

Digital Video

In 1951, researchers Hoban and van Ormer summarized research on instructional films up to that point with the following generalizations:

- People learn from films.
- The use of effective and appropriate films results in more learning in less time and better retention of what is learned.
- Films in combination with other instructional materials are better than either alone.
- Instructional films stimulate other learning activities.
- Films facilitate thinking and problem solving.
- Films are equivalent to a good instructor in communicating facts or demonstrating procedures.

In the late 1970s and through the 1980s, some educators turned to interactive video (stored on videodiscs or laserdiscs), which included both video and still images that could be computer controlled. An analysis of 10 years of research (McNeil and Nelson 1991) found that uses of interactive video to supplement instruction resulted in "higher achievement affects than when interactive video was used in place of traditional forms of instruction" (p. 3). The researchers also concluded that interactive video worked best when it was guided and structured, as opposed to being entirely under the control of the learner.

Recently, an evaluation of a commercial video-streaming library marketed to schools determined that some students who viewed a number of the subject-specific video clips scored higher on content-knowledge tests than did students receiving instruction "in the usual manner" without the video clips (Boster et al. 2006). The gains were not consistent across all age groups and subject areas, however, and authors suggested that possibly the quality of video content suffered in some areas or that too much time had elapsed since some teachers had undergone training on how to teach with the video clips. Both explanations underscore that there's nothing magic about the videos themselves.

Other studies examined how pictures and video can be used most effectively to aid learning, and their results are presented in the following section that provides guidelines for using digital images and video in teaching and learning.

Guidelines for Best Practice

A few practical guidelines for using digital images and video effectively in science instruction can be gleaned from the literature. The guidelines are based on the assumption that the images and video will be viewed on a computer screen, with or without the aid of a computer projector.

(1) Selected photos and videos must specifically illustrate the targeted content and match the instructional goal.

Bransford and colleagues determined that to be effective a picture must provide information about the relations among the concrete elements being described in the text. In addition, they found that pictures best aid in the comprehension of text (as well as in long-term recall, Findahl 1971) when they are closely related to the information provided in the text. Pictures seem to have the greatest effect when they provide a way for people to interpret what they have read or heard, when they provide a means for connecting or organizing the information in the text, or when they help readers verify their understanding of the text.

On the other hand, Levin, Anglin, and Carney (1987) found that pictures serving a primarily decorative purpose had no positive effect and sometimes served as a distraction from learning the target concepts.

Photos can be especially effective when showing students objects they might not otherwise be able to see—such as microscopic organisms and structures, astronomical objects, spatial relationships in ecosystems, and adaptations of plants and wildlife. They may also be helpful with learners for whom English is a second language.

Dale provided excellent advice in his 1969 text on methods for using pictures: "Each picture should accomplish a definite purpose in the lesson. Plan to introduce each item at the proper point—to bring clarity and reality, to suggest a question, to correct a misunderstanding, to concretize a verbalism, and so on" (p. 447).

Likewise, Dale recommended that before using video (or "motion pictures" in his day) teachers should know what they want students to learn—"new facts, relationships, manual skills, judgment, application of film material?"—and select video accordingly. Hoban and van Ormer (1951) noted that movies cannot stand alone to replace the teacher, but movies have specific strengths, especially in terms of reinforcing and extending previous knowledge, attitudes, and motivation.

In summary, use your limited time to find images and video that engage students' attention in the content they need to learn. Don't succumb to the temptation to spend hours looking for cute clipart and fancy PowerPoint backgrounds. Although these may provide aesthetically pleasing visuals, they have little potential to help your students better learn science.

(2) Ensure that students have a meaningful interaction with images or video.

To be fully utilized by students, photos and video require skillful questioning and discussion led by the teacher. A sure way to cut off opportunities for interaction is to point to the subject of an image and tell students what it is. Instead, begin with general questions, like, "Why did I put this image up? What does it have to do with what we're studying?" The difference between good and bad class discussion is often questioning versus telling.

Weidenmann (1989) was concerned that students usually view text as more informative than pictures and that they give even good pictures only a brief glance. Furthermore, he found that a passing reference to a picture in a text (such as, "See Figure 1") is not enough to direct students' attention to the picture. "Most people are convinced that the understanding of pictures requires only a small amount of invested mental effort. As a consequence, one tends to process pictures only superficially" (p. 161). Weidenmann concluded from an exploratory study that learners perceived pictures to be the most beneficial when the text explicitly directed their attention to the pictures' informational aspects.

Weidenmann's findings can also apply to students viewing an image on a screen. Left to their own devices they are likely to consider only the aesthetics of the image and miss the rich information it provides. You may need to guide students in the skill of picture reading, which ranges from simply enumerating objects in a photograph to interpreting and inferring. For example, using an image like the well known "Earth at Night" photo (Figure 1), you can ask questions like,

- What do you see here?
- What is this a picture of?
- Which areas have the most light?
- Why do you think that is?
- Do you think this image represents Earth at an instant in time?

Figure 1.

Earth at night.

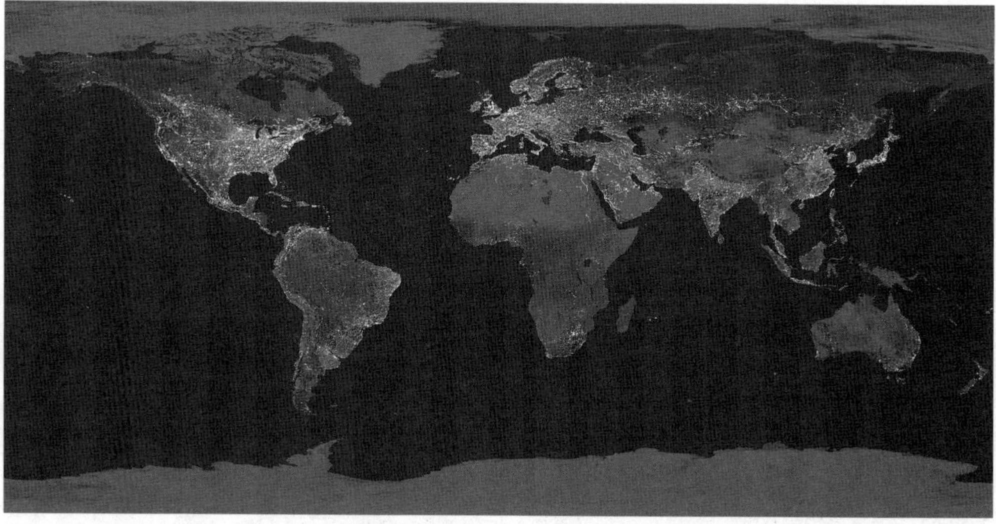

C. MAYHEW AND R. SIMMON (NASA/GSFC), NOAA/NGDC, DMSP DIGITAL ARCHIVE

Discussion before and after showing a video (of any length) is also important. Videos are more effective when, prior to viewing, students are instructed what to look for or what questions will be raised or answered in the video (Dale 1969). These issues should be brought up again after the video in a debriefing session. You'll want to evaluate whether students understood what they saw and whether they learned the content you wanted them to learn or noticed the phenomenon you want to explore further.

(3) Make sure the image or video supplements your good instruction, not replaces it. Video and images should never be used merely as filler or so the teacher can avoid teaching the subject. The mere fact that video and images are easier to obtain doesn't mean they add value to learning. Remember, too, that displaying a video or image in the presence of students does not automatically ensure that students now understand the target concept. Every video clip or image should provide good examples of science content or show students what they could not otherwise see (e.g., different types of volcanoes or the consequences of improper lab procedures). Images do not have to be spectacular to add value to your lesson. In some cases, simple close-up photographs are useful. For instance, a close-up image of a volumetric flask provides a much more realistic view of the meniscus than the typical textbook drawing (see Figure 2).

Figure 2.

Close-up photo showing meniscus.

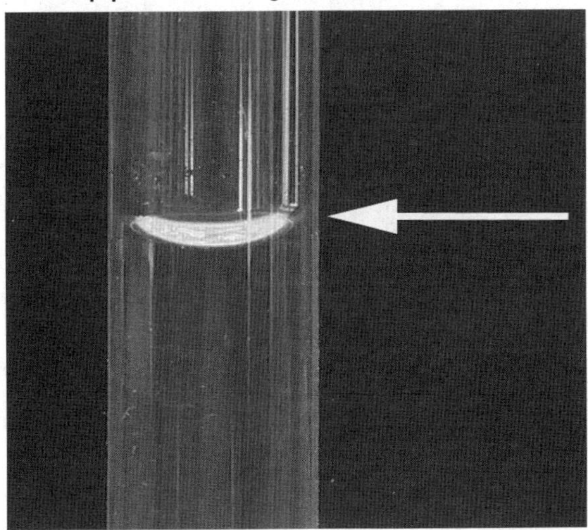

PHOTO BY CHRIS SCHNITTKA

(4) Model appropriate use and attributions of copyrighted digital images and video.
Every teacher should model appropriate use and attributions of digital images and video taken from the web. Web content is not a free-for-all. Images and video are copyrighted just as text is. Although some educational uses fall under "fair use" guidelines, this can be a murky area, so know your school district policies on this issue. Some districts have adopted the Educational Multimedia Fair Use Guidelines, developed in 1996 by the Consortium of College and University Media Centers (Guidelines available online at *www.utsystem.edu/OGC/IntellectualProperty/ccmcguid.htm*).

DIGITAL PHOTO QUALITY

For computer screen or electronic slideshows, the resolution of the final picture (after cropping) needs to be around 72 pixels per inch (ppi). If you want the picture to fill the screen, it should be around 800–1,000 pixels wide at 72 ppi.

Higher resolution means the digital image will take up more file space than necessary. A slide presentation file full of high-resolution photos may become so large that it is difficult to transport it to other computers.

Lower resolution (less than 72 ppi) will result in a blurred image with jagged edges. If you need to enlarge a picture, make sure that the resolution is higher than 72 ppi to begin with, because as you enlarge the picture, the resolution will decrease.

Images can be resized with photo editing programs, like Adobe Photoshop Elements or the GIMP (a free download from the web).

Although these guidelines were never adopted into law, they still provide useful advice. A more simplified summary of the guidelines can be found on the North Carolina Department of Public Instruction website at *www.ncpublicschools.org/copyright1.html*.

Examples of Best Practice

Using Digital Images and Movies as Hooks or Advance Organizers

Figure 3.

Condensation cloud.

U.S. NAVY PHOTO BY ENSIGN JOHN GAY. [990707-N-6483G-001] JULY 7, 1999

Without too much effort (and at no cost!), you can probably find a great photo or movie on the web to introduce about any science topic. Good images or video along with creative questioning can capture students' attention and set the context for their later comprehension of the topic you will discuss.

Digital Images

For example, after some initial instruction on the Doppler effect, you might challenge students with the cloudburst pictured in Figure 3. You might ask students to use what they know about sound waves and compression to explain the conditions or factors that would cause the cloud to be produced by the jet. (For opposing explanations of this effect, see *http://sonicbooms.org/images/F18Condensation.html* and *www.eng.vt.edu/fluids/msc/gallery/conden/pg_sing.htm*.)

Digital Video

Introduce the topic of average velocity by showing a scene from an action movie like *Back to the Future III*, in which characters Doc, Marty, and Clara are accelerating down the railroad tracks on a speeding locomotive toward an unfinished bridge. The locomotive slams through a barricade stating that the track ends in one-fourth mile. Students can use stopwatches to time the duration from when the locomotive hits that sign to when it reaches the end of the track. Since the distance is known from the movie and the time is known from the stopwatches, the average velocity can be calculated. Were they close to the required 88 miles per hour? The height of a large wheel of the locomotive can be estimated; hence, the circumference can be calculated. Knowing the time that it takes for one rotation of the wheel by counting the number of frames, the average velocity can be calculated.

Figure 4

This photo captures the physical reaction taking place when several Mentos candy pieces are dropped into a 2-liter bottle of soda. Carbon dioxide rapidly goes from the dissolved state to the gas state as it nucleates on the microscopic pits on the surface of the candy. Something about the candy dissolving affects the surface tension that normally keeps the bubbles compressed.

PHOTO BY LYNN BELL

Analysis

Digital Images

An observation and inference exercise can help students learn important process skills.[1] Use an interesting photo, like the one in Figure 4 that shows an object or event not immediately recognizable to students. Then have students perform the following steps.

[1] This activity is based on a photo analysis worksheet constructed by the National Archives (*www.archives.gov/education/lessons/worksheets/photo.html*).

VIDEO IN THE PHYSICAL SCIENCE CLASSROOM

In Mr. Fox's physical science class, students video recorded their rocket flights and were challenged to determine how high their rockets flew (without the aid of video analysis software). Here's how they did it: Students knew that at the peak altitude of rocket flight an ejection charge releases the recovery system (usually a parachute or streamers). Students could see the recovery system ejection on the video and also hear the "pop" of the ejection charge. They timed the seconds between seeing the ejection and hearing the charge, then used what they knew about the speed of sound to calculate the peak altitude of the rocket.

Observe: Study the photograph for one minute. Form an overall impression of the photograph and then examine individual items.

Infer: Based on what you have observed, list three things you might infer from this photograph.

Do you think all the other students in the class will make the same inferences you have? Why or why not?

Questions: What questions does this photograph raise in your mind?
Have students share their responses and bring closure with a discussion about differences between observation and inference.

Figure 5.

Final frame used in a movie that shows the position of the model rocket once every three frames, using the boy as the frame of reference for height.

SCREEN CAPTURE OF VIDEO PLAYBACK USING VERNIER LOGGER PRO SOFTWARE.

Digital Video

Video recording students' hands-on activities provides multiple opportunities for analysis. For instance, in a model rocketry project, video can capture the rocket flight, allowing students to later review aspects of the event they may have missed because they were occurring too quickly (see text box, above).

A number of video analysis programs have recently come on the market that allow students to mark an object's location frame by frame on a video to determine velocity, acceleration, and (if mass is known) other values like force, momentum, and potential energies. Students see the video

Figure 6.

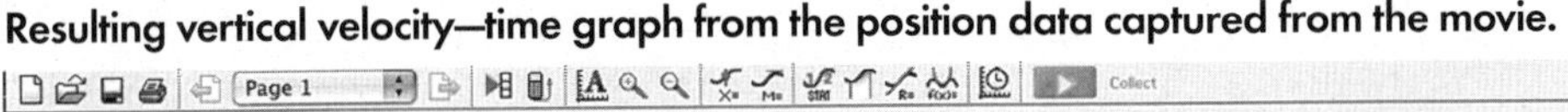

Resulting vertical velocity–time graph from the position data captured from the movie.

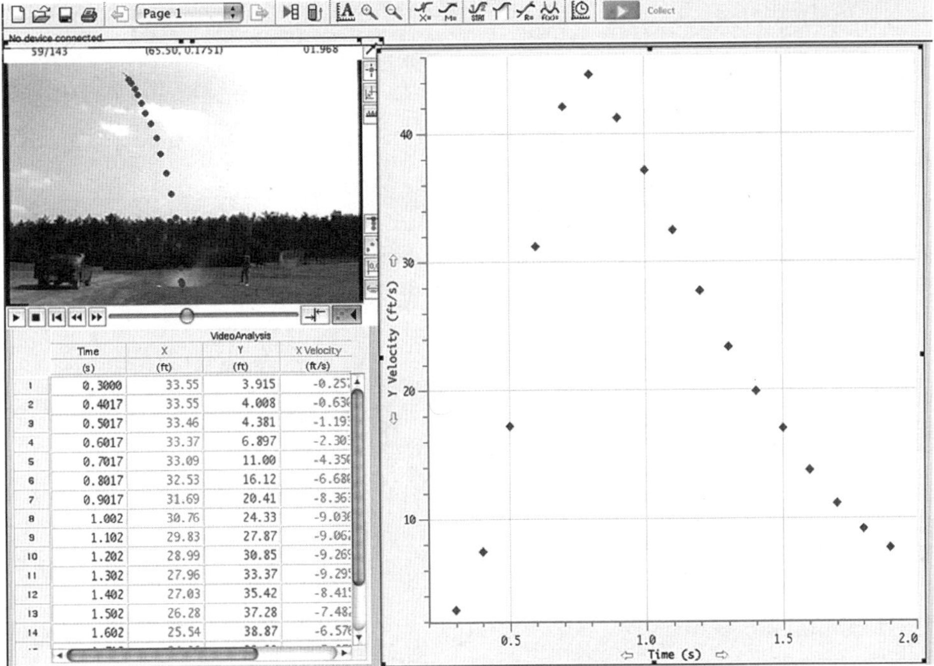

	Time (s)	X (ft)	Y (ft)	X Velocity (ft/s)
1	0.3000	33.55	3.915	-0.25
2	0.4017	33.55	4.008	-0.63
3	0.5017	33.46	4.381	-1.19
4	0.6017	33.37	6.897	-2.30
5	0.7017	33.09	11.00	-4.35
6	0.8017	32.53	16.12	-6.68
7	0.9017	31.69	20.41	-8.36
8	1.002	30.76	24.33	-9.03
9	1.102	29.83	27.87	-9.06
10	1.202	28.99	30.85	-9.26
11	1.302	27.96	33.37	-9.29
12	1.402	27.03	35.42	-8.41
13	1.502	26.28	37.28	-7.48
14	1.602	25.54	38.87	-6.57

SCREEN CAPTURE OF MOTION ANALYSIS USING VERNIER LOGGER PRO SOFTWARE.

playback and a graphical representation of the data side by side on a computer screen (for examples, see Figures 5 and 6). This technology allows students to study two-dimensional motion and multiple objects in motion. Students can make more precise analyses of model rocket flights, and track movement of other objects such as a car going down a ramp, a ball bouncing or tossed into the air, or a person walking or running. For ideas on using video analysis software with probeware, see Chapter 4.

Figure 7.

July 22, 1980 eruption of Mount St. Helens, with Mount Adams, Washington, in the background.

USGS PHOTOGRAPH TAKEN ON JULY 22, 1980, BY JIM VALLANCE.

Seeing Natural Objects Outside Students' Experience

Digital Images

Lots of free images can be found on the web that allow students to see natural objects they might not otherwise be able to view firsthand—fossils, fungi, marine animals, volcanoes, or fault scarps, for example. The following are a few websites with good images for science.

- **Volcano World**
  A collection of volcano photographs from around the Earth and beyond:
  http://volcano.und.edu
- **Erosion: Sediment Is Transported**
  These images show that rocks and sediments get removed from their original locations, building up in some regions and resulting in stripping in other regions:
  www.crewten.com/g_pinto_t2.html
  http://uregina.ca/~sauchyn/geog323/mw.html
- **Fossil Image Galleries, The Virtual Fossil Museum**
  Picture galleries of fossils organized by taxonomy and fossil site:
  http://www.fossilmuseum.net/index.htm
  Additional fossil images can be found on the Fossil Images Archive:
  www.fossilmuseum.net/Education.htm
- **Hubble Site Gallery**
  This official site of the Hubble Space Telescope includes images of deep-space objects and space shuttles:
  http://hubblesite.org/gallery
- **What We Eat . . .**
  Photomicrograph pictures of popular food items, like hamburger, onion, lettuce and potato… or what your food looks like at a cellular level. These would be good to identify similarities and differences between animal and plant cells, and even differences between plant cell structures:
  http://micro.magnet.fsu.edu/micro/gallery/burgersnfries/burgersnfries.html

Digital Video

Especially when you want to engage student thinking about chemical reactions or other events that may be too dangerous, too expensive, or just impossible to do in the class, digital videos can be useful. Good websites for obtaining science videos include the following:

- **Journal of Chemical Education**
  Sample movies from Chemistry Comes Alive:
  http://jchemed.chem.wisc.edu/jcesoft/cca/cca0/sampmovs.htm
- **Miller Single Concept Films in Physics**
  http://physics.kenyon.edu/coolphys/FranklinMiller

- **Science Junction**
  Day and Night—Changes During the Year:
  www.ncsu.edu/sciencejunction/station/experiments/earthkam/simulation/year.html
- **Phases of the Earth as Viewed From the Moon**
  www.ncsu.edu/sciencejunction/phasesofearth.html

Collecting visual data

Digital Images

The following are some ideas for engaging students in collecting their own visual data:

- Create virtual leaf and flower collections: Students can take their own photos (including photos of habitat). Hold an online digital picture scavenger hunt for students who don't have access to natural areas. Compile images into a dichotomous key or field guide to the local flora.
- Record life cycles: Using a digital microscope or camera that can be set to capture images at regular intervals over extended periods of time, photograph a butterfly emerging from its chrysalis, a pet tarantula molting, or a seed germinating. Then use software to convert the still images into a digital video.
- Record long-term events: Create a photo sequence of changing shadows throughout a day or across seasons. Use a digital microscope (or a camera attached to a traditional microscope) to take time-lapse photographs of crystals forming from a drop of salt water and use software to convert the still images into a digital video.
- Take before-and-after pictures of experiments or lab activities.

Digital Video

Students can create a digital video from still images. Using their own digital images or those obtained from the web, students can insert images into the storyboard of a digital video editor. Many of today's tech-savvy students have this software on their home computers and will be adept at adding text, background music, transitions between images, and even narration in their own voice to create a movie synthesizing their understanding of a science concept.

In addition to filming objects in motion for video analysis in physics classes, students can collect video data on animal behavior or other natural phenomena involving movement. A small wireless video camera attached to a bird feeder is a great way to collect data about the types of birds in the area.

Conclusion

The great thing about digital images and video is that you don't need a huge equipment budget and a roomful of computers to take advantage of them. Even with a single computer connected to a projector or television screen and an internet connection, you can have access to a variety of resources for engaging students and helping them learn science concepts.

Using Computer Simulations to Enhance Science Teaching and Learning

Randy L. Bell and Lara K. Smetana

Have you ever been able to have your students vary the force of gravity and determine the effects on an object's motion? Explore nuclear fission at the molecular level and discover whether the daughter atoms are always the same? Move tectonic plates while investigating the differences between divergent and convergent boundaries?

Computer simulations make these types of interactive, authentic, meaningful learning opportunities possible. Learners can observe, explore, recreate, and receive immediate feedback about real objects, phenomena, and processes that would otherwise be too complex, time-consuming, or dangerous.

Broadly defined, computer simulations are computer-generated dynamic models that present theoretical or simplified models of real-world components, phenomena, or processes. They can include animations, visualizations, and interactive laboratory experiences.

In a simulated environment, time changes can be sped up or slowed down; abstract concepts can be made concrete and tacit behaviors visible. Teachers can focus students' attention on learning objectives when real-world environments are simplified, causality of events is clearly explained, and unnecessary cognitive tasks are reduced through a simulation.

Technological advances have increasingly brought instructional digital technologies into the science classroom. Teachers may have greater access to Internet-connected classroom computers, wireless laptop carts, computer projectors, and interactive whiteboards than ever before. As you consider how these resources can be used to enhance science teaching and learning, you may find yourself turning often to computer simulations, especially since they are tools frequently used by scientists in their daily work.

You are likely to find at least one simulation for any science concept represented in the National Science Education Standards. Many of these simulations can be accessed online (some for a fee, like at *www.ExploreLearning.com*[1]; others at no cost, such as on the PBS You Try It site, *www.pbs.org/wgbh/aso/tryit*). Other more complex simulations with large underlying databases (like Starry Night) are available as commercial software. This chapter seeks to describe how computer simulations can support student learning in science as well as strategies for choosing and appropriately incorporating them in the classroom.

What the Research Says

Simulations have been around practically since the advent of computers, and researchers have been looking at classroom uses of simulations for over 20 years. The following two sections describe what is known about the effectiveness of computer simulations for supporting science teaching and learning and highlighting ways that simulations can be best used to do so. The overview of the literature provides a summary of the past two decades of research, including a discussion of several seminal pieces. Finally, a set of guidelines presents best practices drawn from this body of literature.

Researchers studying the use of simulations in the classroom have reported positive findings overall. The literature indicates that simulations can be effective in developing content knowledge and process skills, as well as in promoting more complicated goals such as inquiry and conceptual change. Gains in student understanding and achievement have been reported in general science process skills and across specific subject areas, including physics, chemistry, biology, and Earth and space science (Kulik 2002).

Although conventional instructional materials such as textbooks present two-dimensional representations, simulations can offer three-dimensional manipulatives that bring the subject matter to life. Visualization results in the development of mental constructs that allow one to think about, describe, and explain objects, phenomena, and processes in a more true-to-life form. These are just the habits of mind scientists rely upon in their daily work. For example, after comparing simulated and hands-on dissection labs, Akpan and Andre (2000) concluded, "The flexibility of these kinds of environments makes learning right and wrong answers less important than learning to solve problems and make decisions. Simulations promote learning about what-ifs and possibilities, not about certainties" (p. 18).

Studies assessing the impact of simulations on process skill development, such as identifying variables, measuring, graphing, interpreting data, and designing experiments, have shown computer simulations to be equally as or more valuable

[1] The ExploreLearning site at the time of this writing offers a free 30-day trial period for the entire collection of science and mathematics simulations. In addition, individuals may use any simulation for five minutes a day at no charge.

than traditional methods. For example, a study by Geban, Askar, and Ozkan (1992) investigated the effects of a computer-simulated experiment on chemistry achievement and process skills. The researchers found greater student achievement with simulated labs than with hands-on labs.

A study by Mintz (1993) found that students were successful in designing, implementing, and analyzing the results of three ecological problems, noting improvement even as the inquiry tasks became increasingly complex. Students also began employing more formal analytical strategies, rather than relying on trial and error.

Trundle and Bell (2005) described students' conceptual understandings about lunar concepts before and after instruction with planetarium simulations. Results indicated that students learned more about moon shapes and sequences, as well as causes of moon phases, by using the computer simulations than by making actual nightly observations and studying nature alone. The ability to make many more observations using the program, the ease of making and testing predictions, and the consistency and accuracy of student measurements contributed to the dramatic improvements in student understanding.

The past 20 years of research indicates that students' misconceptions in science are prevalent and tenacious. Thus, the process of conceptual change is an ongoing challenge in science education. Computer simulations have demonstrated the potential to facilitate this process by highlighting students' misconceptions and presenting plausible scientific conceptions. For instance, using computerized interactive laboratory simulations, learners can confront their beliefs by working with real data, experiencing discrepant events preselected by the program, or forming and testing multiple hypotheses of their own (Gorsky and Finegold 1992; Tao and Gunstone 1999; Trundle and Bell 2005).

Overall, the research shows that interaction with computer simulations resulted in measurable achievement gains and indicates that simulations are equally, if not more, effective than traditional methods. Access to multiple representations of phenomena, the ability to manipulate the environment, ease of posing and testing multiple hypotheses, and ability to control variables are consistently cited in the research as contributing to the effectiveness of computer simulations. Other noted benefits to consider when comparing instructional approaches include cost and time efficiency, student enthusiasm, high engagement, and on-task behavior while working with simulations. Effectiveness, however, varies based on design features, support measures, and sequencing of simulation activities within the curriculum (Bayraktar 2002; Kulik 2002).

Guidelines for Best Practice

Effective uses of computer simulations in the science classroom are abundant and as varied as the teachers who use them. You might incorporate a simulation of cellular mitosis into a lecture to illustrate the new concept; a dissection simulation may serve as a precursor to a hands-on dissection lab; student pairs may build atoms of elements in the alkali metals family while deducing periodic trends; ChemBalancer (a program for balancing chemical equations, available at *http://funbasedlearning.com/chemistry/chembalancer/default.htm*) may serve as an interactive homework review. As teachers respond to increased access to digital technologies such as interactive whiteboards, more and more creative uses of simulations appear. However, students can benefit from simulations even with a basic classroom setup of a single teacher computer connected to a projector.

Remember that technologies like computer simulations are tools to support learning. As with any other educational tool, the effectiveness of computer simulations is limited by the ways in which they are used. Certainly, instructional strategies proven to support meaningful learning should be adhered to when using computer simulations or any other digital technologies. Students should be actively engaged in the acquisition of knowledge and encouraged to take responsibility for their own learning; content should be placed in the context of the real world and connected to their own lives. In order to maximize the potential of computer simulations to enhance meaningful science learning, we have proposed the following guidelines, representing a synthesis of the recommendations from science educators, researchers, and developers.

(1) Use computer simulations to supplement, not replace, other instructional modes. Computer simulations should be used in conjunction with hands-on labs and activities that also address the concepts targeted by the simulation. Indeed, one study has indicated that simulations used in isolation were ineffective (Hsu and Thomas 2002). When preceding a hands-on activity, a simulation may familiarize students with a concept under a focused environment.

For example, chemistry students might become familiar with titration virtually (using a titration simulator like the one created by Yue-Ling Wong at *www.wfu.edu/~ylwong/chem/titrationsimulator/index.html*) before doing a hands-on titration lab. When an interactive simulation is used as a follow-up, students can continue investigations of questions and manipulations of variables that would otherwise be impossible under the constraints of the lab equipment or class schedule. For example, after gaining a basic understanding of the Doppler effect through real-life examples, a Doppler simulation allows students to visualize the movement of sound waves and even develop an explanation of a sonic boom (see, for example, the Absorb Physics courseware site: *www.crocodile-clips.com/absorb/AP5/sample/040103.html*)

When planning for instruction using simulations, ask yourself: "How can this simulation be used to extend what I am doing in the classroom?" "What can I do with this simulation that I would not otherwise be able to do?" "Can using this simulation give me more time to spend on something else?" Integrating simulations into the curriculum also ensures that connections to domain knowledge and real-world applications are made explicit. As with any instructional technology, computer simulations should be chosen to meet your objectives and teach the content (Flick and Bell 2000).

(2) Keep instruction student centered.

By exposing complex concepts and abstract phenomena, computer simulations offer the opportunity to engage students in higher-level thinking and challenge them to struggle with new ideas. Lessons involving computer simulations should remain student-centered and inquiry-based to ensure that learning is focused on meaningful understandings, not rote memorization. Depending on your instructional objectives and classroom arrangement, the student groupings and computer setups will vary. You may choose to integrate simulations such as Stellarium (a free open-source virtual planetarium available at *www.stellarium.org*) into your lectures as a teacher-led demonstration, or students may work in a lab setting individually or in small groups with programs such as Net Frog (an interactive virtual dissection available at *http://curry.edschool.virginia.edu/go/frog*).

When simulations are teacher led, students should be actively engaged through questioning, prediction generation and testing, and conclusion drawing (Soderberg 2003). Connections made to their own lives make the learning more authentic and meaningful. Closure to the lesson is as important for simulated activities as for conventional activities; have students restate their understandings and consider real-world applications.

When students work with simulations individually or in small groups, discussion and collaboration among teachers and peers should be fostered. Regardless of the implementation you choose, students should be prompted to form and test their own hypotheses and justify their decisions. By encouraging reflection on their actions and decision-making, you can help expose student misconceptions, allowing for conceptual change and development. Students can then begin to monitor and take responsibility for their own learning.

(3) Point out the limitations of simulations.

By definition, simulations are simplified models of the real world. Although it is necessary for students to accept the simulated environment as an intelligible and plausible representation of reality, it is also critical that students realize the differences between the simulation and reality. Without understanding a model's limitations, students may form misconceptions. This distinction is particularly important when dealing with submicroscopic objects or invisible phenomena. For instance, it is important to stress that protons, neutrons, and electrons are not actually red, blue, and yellow as they may be depicted in a simulated model of the atom. Attention should also be given to scale and timeframe when they are altered for the sake of simplification. For instance, students should understand that, in reality, volcanoes take hundreds of years to form, not a matter of seconds (as it appears in simulations like the following on the PBS You Try It site: *www.pbs.org/wgbh/aso/tryit/tectonics*). A discussion of why scientists use models and the role they have in scientific inquiry would be a valuable component of any lesson involving simulations (Harrison and deJong 2005).

(4) Make content, not technology, the focus.
When it comes to computer simulations, the range of accessibility is as wide as the topics spanned. Although some simulations are extremely user friendly and self-explanatory, others require a good deal of time to become familiar with. If students are to be using them on their own, they must understand how the program operates. Otherwise, they may get bogged down with logistical issues rather than remaining focused on the educational objectives. To avoid this dilemma, you may choose to lead the class through the simulation as a demonstration, ensuring the type of student engagement described previously. Even when the program is designed for independent student use, be sure to familiarize your students with its features, discuss its limitations, model its use, and provide access to any additional domain knowledge and tools that might facilitate their work. This is particularly important when using highly open-ended simulations that do not provide support structures, such as tutorials, guided questions, or help menus. For example, begin by working through an initial problem as a class, allowing students to steer you through manipulations of parameters. Then, students can work through subsequent problems independently, with your scaffolding. Certainly the most effective type of support and means of providing it are dependent upon the ability and needs of your students and the specific learning goals.

Examples of Best Practice

Activities using four highly interactive simulations are described in this section: StarryNight and ExploreLearning simulations are commercial, and the Virtual Optics Bench and Atom Builder are available free online.

Virtual Planetarium Software

Teaching an astronomy unit over the course of a few weeks during daylight hours in a typical classroom setting is a formidable challenge. No wonder students have so many alternative conceptions! Virtual planetarium simulations offer one solution. They allow students to investigate astronomy from any perspective, from any place on Earth, at any point in time, under the ideal conditions of a controlled environment (i.e., no obstructions, clouds, or fog). For example, a commercial virtual planetarium program called StarryNight can be used in a class demonstration to answer the question "How do stars appear to move in the sky?" (Figure 1) Although it by no means replaces the experience of an evening field trip to view the stars, you can select your own location, current date, and time to keep the investigation authentic and meaningful to students.

Students can make preliminary predictions, then view and review the motion

Figure 1.

Screen capture from Starry Night virtual planetarium software

of the stars through the sky. You can engage students in conversation about their observations, having them generate additional questions and revise their predictions, then develop their own definition of circumpolar stars. By further investigating Polaris, Ursa Major, and the Big Dipper from the equator and the North Pole, for instance, students can notice differences in the apparent motion of the stars, depending on their viewpoint. Discuss with students possible explanations, leading students to understand that the apparent movement of the stars is due to the Earth's rotation. Then encourage students to make their own observations of the stars in the night sky from home and share their findings in class over the course of the next week. (Students should be made aware that distortions on the edges of the Moon and other planetary bodies result from attempting to represent a three-dimensional object on a two-dimensional computer screen.

Virtual Optics Bench

Virtual Optics Bench is a java applet that takes instruction using ray diagrams to a new level. (This OpticsApplet is available free online at *http://webphysics.davidson.edu/Applets/optics4/default.html* or in a larger format at *www.hazelwood.k12.mo.us/~grichert/optics/intro.html*) You and your students have access to concave and convex lenses and mirrors, point light sources, culminated light sources, and objects for showing real and virtual images with the click of a mouse. In this dynamic environment, students are able to visualize and investigate the effects of changing parameters, such as the focal length of a lens or the location of a light source.

A lesson may begin with students experimenting with a variety of lenses, noticing differences in the appearance of an image when viewed through lenses of various curvatures (Figure 2). After introducing the term *focal length* as a description of how curved a lens is, pose the question, "What impact does focal length have on the position and size of the image formed?" Initial qualitative observations can be extended to a more in-depth quantitative analysis using the Virtual Optics Bench. Although doing so with the traditional approach of drawing ray diagrams is time-consuming and tedious for students, this inquiry investigation is easily accomplished with the computer simulation. Students can make and test their predictions using the Virtual Optics Bench.

Figure 2.

Screen capture from the Virtual Optics Bench.

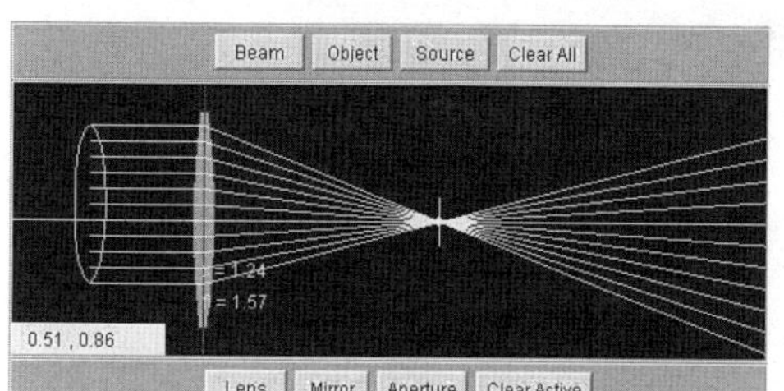

Insert an object (shown as an arrow) and a convex lens on the workbench. Draw students' attention to how the lens refracts the light rays to form an image of the object. At this point, it is important to ensure students understand that the ray diagrams shown are only a simplification of reality and that light given off by an object actually extends infinitely in all directions. Drag the lens to change the focal length. The size and location of the object and image are measured by the program, allowing for both quantitative and qualitative analysis. The investigation can be easily extended to include concave lenses and mirrors. At the end of the unit, you may choose to include screen shots of the virtual workspace in your assessments.

ExploreLearning Mouse Breeding

Rarely do students have the opportunity to perform genetics experiments in the classroom, due to lack of time and resources. Using the interactive online Mouse Breeding simulation at *www.ExploreLearning.com*, students can perform virtual genetic experiments.[2] Students can use this simulation to explore questions like, "Can dark-haired

[2] This site requires a subscription for long-term use, but you may take advantage of the free 30-day trial period.

parents produce light-haired offspring?" The Mouse Breeding simulation is appropriate for students to use on their own in the computer lab, individually or in small groups. (You should provide guidance on how to operate the program's features and model a few preliminary crosses as a class demonstration.) Students should keep track of their results, including parent genotypes, Punnett squares, and phenotype ratios, in a lab notebook.

Students can breed various pairs of mice, making predictions first and then running simulated trials (Figure 3). Experiments might include pairing two black-fur mice, two white-fur mice, a purebred black-fur mouse with a purebred white-fur mouse, and two of the resulting hybrid mice. Students will discover that the recessive white fur trait returns, and you can discuss with them why the experimental outcomes do not always match those of the Punnett square and direct students back to the initial question.

Figure 3.

Screen capture from ExploreLearning Mouse Breeding gizmo.

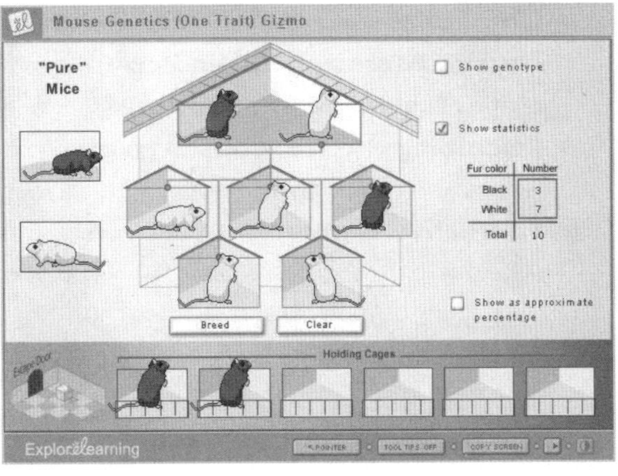

For a more detailed description of this activity, see the TeacherLink website (*www.teacherlink.org/content/science/instructional/activities/genetics/home.html*).

Atom Builder

Did you ever think you would be able to take your class inside an atom? Atom Builder, an interactive Bohr model (available free online at the PBS You Try It site: *www.pbs.org/wgbh/aso/tryit/atom/#*), challenges students to build neutral atoms out of elementary particles (Figure 4).

Figure 4.

Screen capture from Atom Builder simulation.

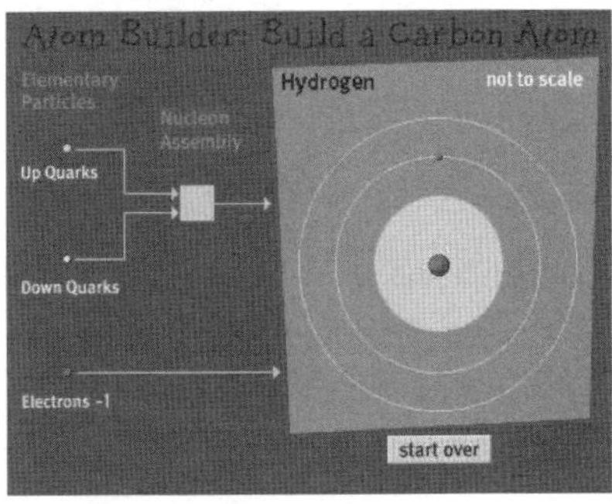

You might begin an activity by asking students what would need to be added in order to change a hydrogen atom into a helium atom. Raise questions such as, "What do you think will happen if three up quarks are put together in the Nucleon Assembly area?" or "Could an electron be placed in the outer energy level?" Encourage students to pose and test their own questions as the class builds other atoms. Throughout, students should explain their decisions, take notice of and reflect on the consequences. As an assessment, have students explain how an

MORE GOOD SIMULATIONS ON THE WEB

- **Learning Science:** A vast collection of animations, simulations, and web-based resources for all subject areas *(www.learningscience.org/index.htm)*
- **Visual Elements:** A visual representation of the Periodic Table *(www.chemsoc.org/viselements)*
- **Virtual Chemistry Lab:** A fully stocked virtual chemistry lab *(www.chemcollective.org/vlab/vlab.php)*
- **OhmZone:** A virtual circuit board *(www.article19.com/shockwave/oz.htm)*
- **Physics Education Technology:** A collection of interactive simulations of physical phenomena *(www.colorado.edu/physics/phet/web-pages/index.html)*
- **Cell Biology Animations:** A collection of animations for a variety of topics, from DNA replication to photosynthesis *(www.johnkyrk.com/index.html)*
- **Interactive Human Body:** An interactive exploration of the human organs, muscles, skeleton, and nervous systems *(www.bbc.co.uk/science/humanbody/body/interactives/3djigsaw_02/index.shtml?skeleton)*

atom changes from one element to another, what is the balance between protons and electrons, and what constitutes a stable atom. Students should also be able to compare the composition of neutrons and protons.

During the lesson closure, it is important to point out that the Bohr model has been replaced by a more complex quantum model of the atom. Your students may find it interesting to research how contributions of scientists like Werner Heisenberg, Louis de Broglie, Erwin Schrodinger, and Wolfgang Pauli working during the 1920s marked a profound shift in the way scientists thought about the atom.

Conclusion

Computer simulations have the potential to enhance the way you teach and your students learn. They allow you to bring even the most abstract concepts to life for your students and incorporate otherwise impossible or impractical experiences into your daily instruction. When used in conjunction with the guidelines presented here, your students will be engaged in inquiry, further develop their knowledge and conceptual understanding of the content, gain meaningful practice with scientific process skills, and confront their misconceptions. Additionally, they will gain scientific habits-of-mind (such as the ability to visualize, contemplate, and explain complex concepts and phenomena) that are both encouraged in the recent reform documents and necessary for future careers in science.

CHAPTER 4

Probeware Tools for Science Investigations

John C. Park

You may have noticed that electronic data collection devices are everywhere these days—at the doctor's office, in the grocery store, on construction sites, and in your students' hands after school (i.e., cell phones with cameras).

Electronic data collection devices should be similarly visible in the school science classroom. Measurement is one of the basic science process skills. Electronic data collection tools can not only help with measurement, but they can facilitate development of the integrated science process skills of interpreting data and formulating models.

Probeware is the general term used for probes and software that can be used with microprocessors (computer, calculator, palm device, etc.) to make scientific measurements. The probes consist of transducers, which are devices that convert physical quantities into electrical quantities. For example, a transducer called a thermistor changes resistance as temperature changes. Because the specific characteristics of the transducer are known, these devices can be calibrated so that microprocessors can convert the measured electrical quantities into meaningful data.

A full collection of probeware can require much of a school's science budget. Collect probeware gradually as you determine how the probes might be used in your classroom or school. The basic software and beginning probe package costs between $40 and $500, depending on the type of probe, interface, and software. If you don't have the budget for multiple probeware lab stations, many of the explorations could be accomplished through teacher demonstration. The learning curve of the software depends on how the software is to be used. I tend not to learn all the functions of a software package; I learn to use only the ones I need, so the learning curve for basic measurements and saving of data is minimal.

The software that instructs the microprocessor can be designed to promote maximum usability. For example, Vernier Software and Technology provides an interface that can simultaneously collect data from four analog inputs (such as temperature probes) and two digital inputs (such as photogates). Vernier also provides the software that automatically determines which probes are plugged into the system (see *www.vernier.com*).

Software is available for computers, calculators, and handheld devices. The user can select the type of experiment, sampling rate, and length of experiment using the software. The software can display the collected data in tabular or in graphic form. Some vendors include data analysis software in their probeware packages. This software allows users to find, for example, the curve of best fit for the data, the slope of the curve at a specific point, or the area under the curve. PASCO (*www.pasco.com*) provides specialized probeware that can be connected to computers wirelessly using Bluetooth technology.

Following is a list of variables that can be measured using various probes:

Acceleration
Altitude
Barometric pressure
Blood pressure
Charge
Carbon dioxide concentration
Concentration of solutions
Conductivity
Current
Dissolved oxygen content
Force
EKG
Flow rate
Gas pressure
Heart rate
Select Ions
Lung volume
Magnetic field strength
Motion
Oxygen concentration
pH
Photogate timing
Radiation
Relative humidity
Respiration rate
Rotary motion
Salinity
Sound frequency
Sound intensity
Soil moisture
Spectra
Temperature
Turbidity
UV light
Visible light
Voltage

The power of probeware is real-time data collection. However, there is only one time-based activity in which pupils can look at the collected data as the exploration continues: using the motion detector while walking, trying to match preexisting graphs. For most other explorations, the users begin the data collection, turn their attention to the event to watch it to completion, and then turn back to the computer or handheld device to see the results. The next generation of probeware merges visualization with analysis, by synchronizing the collected data and resulting graph with a movie of the event. Pupils can scroll across the graph and view the movie simultaneously, stopping and starting or replaying critical regions of the graph to see exactly what is happening in the event during interesting points on the graph.

What the Research Says

The first study of probeware with children was conducted by Tinker and Barclay and published in 1982. The researchers reported that this was the "first indication of the power of kinesthetic real-time interactions to lead to understandings of abstract representations" (Tinker 2004, p. 7). In this study, the short exposure of pupils to the apparatus helped them gain an intuitive understanding of decimal numbers.

Brassel (1987) reported that the simultaneous display of the real-time data resulted in significant learning, whereas a delayed display of the data did not. The use of the displayed data to encourage pupil learning was confirmed in a study by Russell, Lucas, and McRobbie (2003). They ascertained that "students used the display, almost exclusively, as representing the experimental phenomena or task problem" (p. 225), "the nature of the display was supportive of a deep approach to learning" (p. 229), "students critically evaluated the appearance of the graphic display" (p. 230), and "the kinematics graphic display supported students' working memory" (p. 234).

Laboratory activities using probeware are not inherently inquiry activities, as the probeware could be used in "cookbook" fashion. Royuk and Brooks (2003), however, found that when probeware was used in an inquiry-based manner, learning was increased compared to traditional cookbook labs in a college physics class. Slykhuis (2004) demonstrated that inquiry-based curriculum incorporating the use of probeware could be effectively delivered over the web to high school physics pupils.

Guidelines for Best Practice

Probeware should not be used merely to reduce the pressure to use more technology in your teaching. Each use of any teaching method or technology should have a solid rationale for its use. In many cases using a thermometer to make a single measurement in the school science laboratory is more efficient than dragging out the probes. However, if you need to find the change in the temperature over a long period of time, it would be to your advantage to have the computer do the work for you.

(1) Use the tool when it will give you the best data.

Sometimes the probeware offers you a way to collect and analyze data you could not otherwise investigate. For example, you might be able to investigate a pure sound wave by using an oscilloscope. However, most affordable oscilloscopes have no way to capture and save the waveform data. You could take a picture of the screen for later analysis, and you may be able to pick out the fundamental waveform to calculate the frequency based on the timescale of the scope. However, an easier way would be to use a microphone probe to collect the waveform data and use software that will analyze the complex waveform into its component waveforms.

(2) Use probeware when finding a mathematical relationship among measured variables is desired.

The basic premise for the study of science through modeling is to collect data to find relationships among variables being studied. For example, instead of giving students equations from a book, they could generate equations from data they collect with probeware. A motion detector could be used to measure the motion of a cart moving down a ramp. The best curve that fits the collected data from a position-time graph of the event would give the same kinematics equations listed in a textbook. From the mathematical relationships they discover, students can create mathematical models of the phenomena that can be tested. Good probeware will allow users to discover mathematical relationships between variables through curve fitting of the data.

(3) Use probeware when short data collection time is an issue, and incorporate digital video when a view of the event with the data is essential for understanding of the phenomena.

Some events happen so quickly that it is difficult to make measurements using conventional methods. For example, some collisions last only a fraction of a second, and no spring scale will be successfully used. You need an instrument that has a high sampling rate and can measure over short time periods. The same problem exists when you try to measure the force of a rocket engine. However, probeware is able to make such measurements and give you additional data regarding the total impulse of the rocket. In addition, you could create a digital videotape of the event and synchronize the movie with the data, which allows students to see the event exactly when the data is being collected, one instant at a time.

Examples of Best Practice

Probeware can be used in a number of science topic areas to engage students in inquiry learning. Probeware tools allow students to investigate phenomena that are not the usual part of the school science curriculum. The duration of the event under investigation is not a problem since the computer can collect data from rapid events or from events that take days for completion. The large variety of probes now available gives students maximum measurement ability. Here are a few examples of some nontraditional investigations that can be explored using probeware.

Which Freezes Faster?

Ask your students how many of them have been told that hot water freezes faster than cold water. Do they think it's true? Why or why not? Then challenge them to use temperature probes to determine the veracity of this commonly held belief.

Three probes will be needed for this experiment: one centered in the container of hot water, one centered in the container of cold water, and one as a control in the airspace in the freezer. Students can place the temperature probes in the water samples being tested and place them in the freezer. The freezer door will seal around the temperature probe wire when the door is closed. Suggest that students set the software to collect about 24 hours worth of data, with a sampling rate of one sample per minute. Make sure they note which probe is in which environment.

After initial collection of the data, more questions may surface, especially when the graph does not produce what is predicted. For example, the graph in Figure 1 was obtained using a Vernier Lab Pro interface and three stainless steel temperature probes. Probe 1 was in initial warm water (Container A), Probe 2 was in initial cool water (Container B), and Probe 3 measured the air temperature in the freezer compartment.

Figure 1.

Screen capture of temperature measurements in a freezer over a 24-hour period.

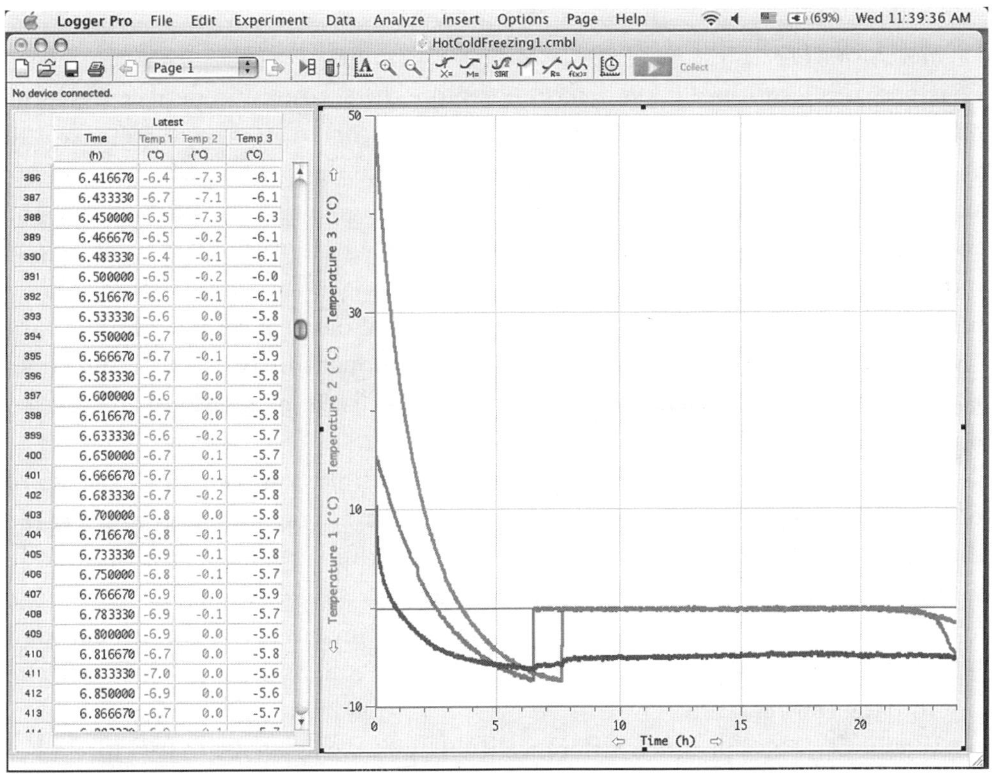

	Latest			
	Time (h)	Temp 1 (°C)	Temp 2 (°C)	Temp 3 (°C)
386	6.416670	-6.4	-7.3	-6.1
387	6.433330	-6.7	-7.1	-6.1
388	6.450000	-6.5	-7.3	-6.3
389	6.466670	-6.5	-0.2	-6.1
390	6.483330	-6.4	-0.1	-6.1
391	6.500000	-6.5	-0.2	-6.0
392	6.516670	-6.6	-0.1	-6.1
393	6.533330	-6.6	0.0	-5.8
394	6.550000	-6.7	0.0	-5.9
395	6.566670	-6.7	-0.1	-5.9
396	6.583330	-6.7	0.0	-5.8
397	6.600000	-6.6	0.0	-5.9
398	6.616670	-6.7	0.0	-5.8
399	6.633330	-6.6	-0.2	-5.7
400	6.650000	-6.7	0.1	-5.7
401	6.666670	-6.7	0.1	-5.8
402	6.683330	-6.7	-0.2	-5.8
403	6.700000	-6.8	0.0	-5.8
404	6.716670	-6.8	-0.1	-5.7
405	6.733330	-6.9	-0.1	-5.8
406	6.750000	-6.8	-0.1	-5.7
407	6.766670	-6.9	0.0	-5.9
408	6.783330	-6.9	-0.1	-5.7
409	6.800000	-6.9	0.0	-5.6
410	6.816670	-6.7	0.0	-5.8
411	6.833330	-7.0	0.0	-5.6
412	6.850000	-6.9	0.0	-5.6
413	6.866670	-6.7	0.0	-5.7

The probe started at the highest temperature (48°C) was the one in Container A, the probe started at midrange (15°C) measured the water in Container B, and the probe started at the lowest temperature (10°C) measured the air in the freezer compartment. The air temperature was initially above freezing due to having the door open when placing the probes and plastic containers holding 250 ml of water into the freezer.

Note that the water temperatures continued to drop past 0°C until it stopped at −7°C. At 6.5 hours into the data collection, the water in Container B jumped to 0° C, the freezing point of water, in less than 1 minute. At a little over 1 hour later, the same thing happened to the water in Container A, jumping from −7°C to 0°C. Near the end of the data collection period, the temperature of the water in Container B began to decrease to the ambient temperature of the air in the freezer, followed by the temperature of the water in the Container A. In my investigation it appears that the cooler water froze first. Have students try to locate on their graph where the phase change occurred. (Hint: A web search on "supercooled water" might help.)

Students may find some other results in addition to answering their original question. Other follow-up questions to ask include the following: Do the containers make a difference? Dissolved gases? Low temperature gradient? Would putting the water samples outside in a cold winter night instead of the freezer change the results?

Volume Under Pressure

A gas pressure sensor is a good device to explore the relationship between volume and pressure. Set the syringe (included with the sensor) to 10 ml and connect it to the gas pressure sensor. Set the software to measure the "event with entry" (this means that you can adjust the volume of the syringe to a specific amount, and the probe continually reads the pressure). Once you have the syringe set, enter your volume setting (10ml). Adjust the volume of the syringe to another specific volume and continue the data collection. This point-by-point data collection continues until you have collected all the desired points. The amount of gas in the syringe does not change as the volume changes; therefore, you will see the relationship between volume and pressure.

As shown on the graph (Figure 2), there is definitely a pattern in the set of points collected in my investigation. The software gives you an option to select the best curve to fit these data points. The inverse function, $y = A/x$ works quite well. With the measured variables, this equates to Pressure = *A*/Volume, or Pressure × Volume = *A*. So what is the meaning of *A*? The resulting curve fit gives the constant a value of 1,004. The constant still has no meaning. Perhaps there is something else built into the constant.

Would there be a pressure difference if the system was cooled to 0°C instead of 22°C? Perhaps temperature is a part of the constant. There is a lot more to explore to identify the "variables" still within the "constant" as identified in this mathematical model.

Figure 2.

Relationship of volume and pressure.

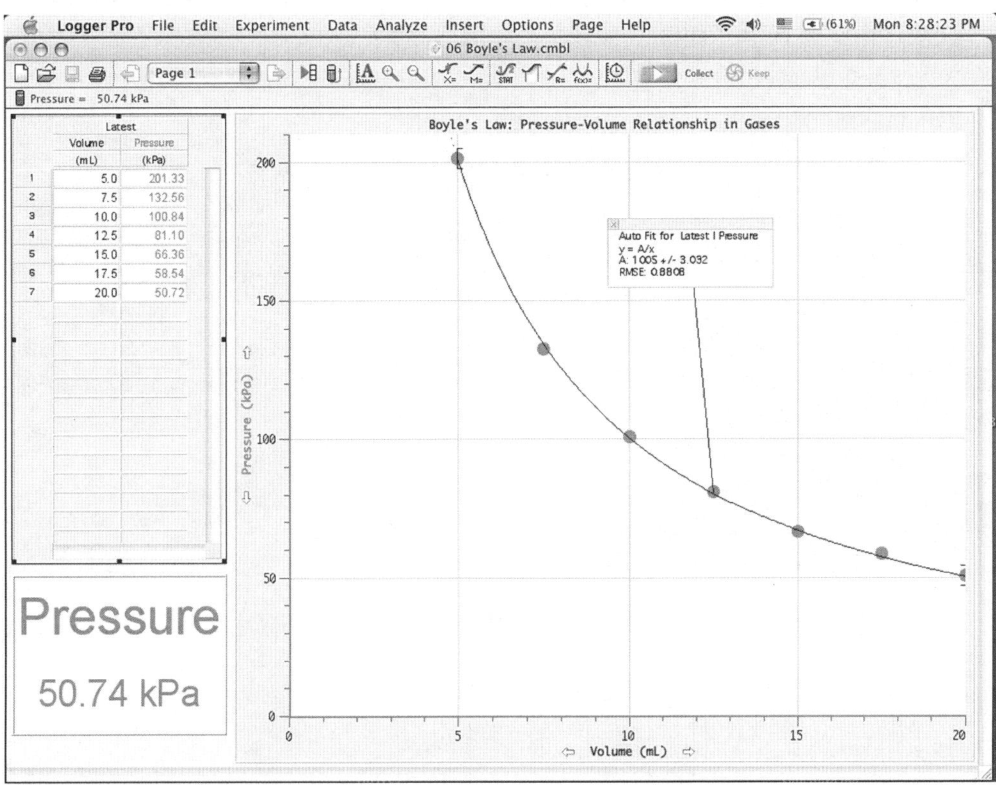

Rocket Engine Forces

Some measurements cannot be done easily any other way but through the use of probeware, and this activity presents one such example. Building and flying model rockets is a common activity in physical science classes. These rockets use disposable solid propellant engines, and the force the engine produces is a key variable in determining the acceleration and peak altitude of a particular rocket. Students can find their own measurements of the force of a rocket engine while it is burning in a static state. They simply need a force probe to measure force over time and synchronized video and software, such as Vernier's Logger Pro.

Place an inverted rocket engine through a copper tube held fast to a ring stand by a clamp (see image in Figure 3). Place the end of the engine against a copper tube end cap, which is resting on a force probe. Use an aluminum pie pan to protect the force probe from the engine blast. Begin video recording, set the computer to begin collecting the data, then ignite the rocket. After the event, the data file is saved in the computer. The resulting Quicktime movie can be imported into the Logger Pro environment and time synchronized to the collected data.

Your data may look something like the data in Figure 3. In this example, data were collected at a rate of 200 points per second (0.005 seconds per point). Ask students what was the force of the peak thrust and how long did it last? How long did the entire force last and what was the average force?

Figure 3.

Force of a C6-4 Estes rocket engine as measured by a force probe.

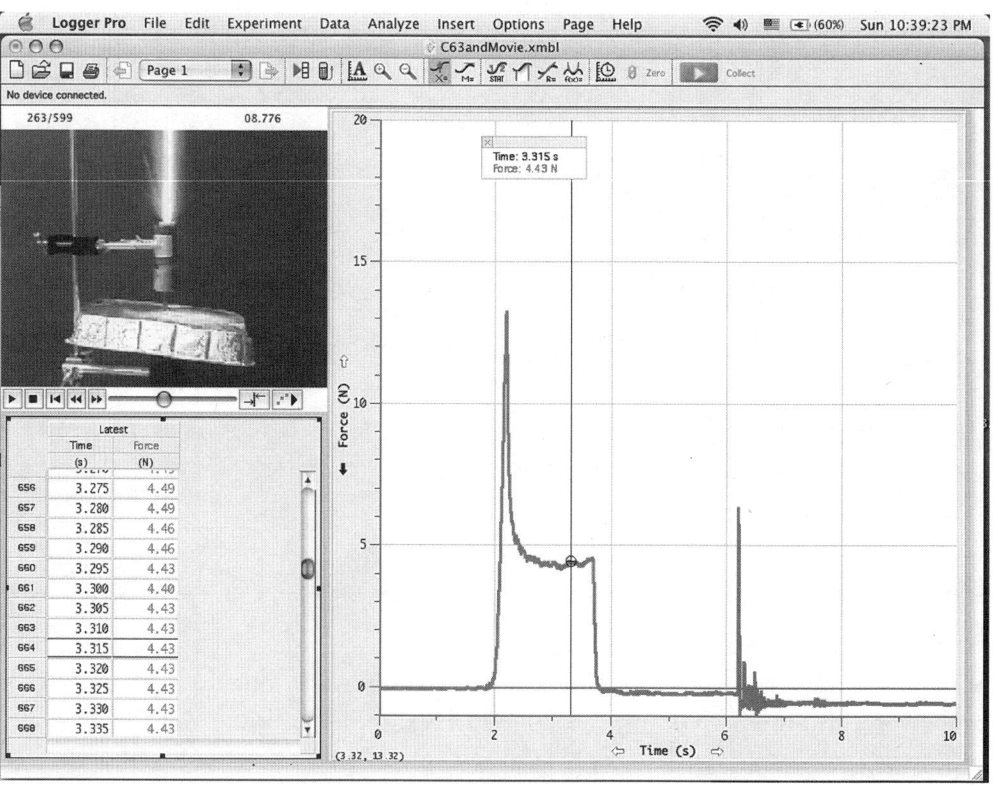

As you drag the cursor across the graph, the data point in the data table is highlighted, and the corresponding incident in the video is displayed. Have students compare the image in the video to the data on the graph. Ask them questions about what is happening at various points during the event and why.

The cursor on the graph is on the plateau range of the force. Notice the burning of the engine in the corresponding frame of the movie shown in the upper left corner of the screen shot. What would be seen in the frame when the cursor is moved across the graph past the plateau? Does the rocket engine quit burning? Move the cursor further to the right where the next sharp peak is located. This instant in time shows the point at which the "ejection" charge stored in the opposite end of the engine is ignited. This charge is used to eject the parachute in the rocket for a slower descent.

Figure 4 illustrates another data analysis option the software has. The user can select a certain range in the *x* data to calculate the area under the curve. In this case, the area is 8.4 newton*seconds. This represents the force * time that the force acted. This is called impulse, and gives us an idea of the change of momentum of the object while the net force was applied. Students can explore many aspects of science using the same data set.

Figure 4.

Screen shot of the measurement of the area under the engine impulse curve.

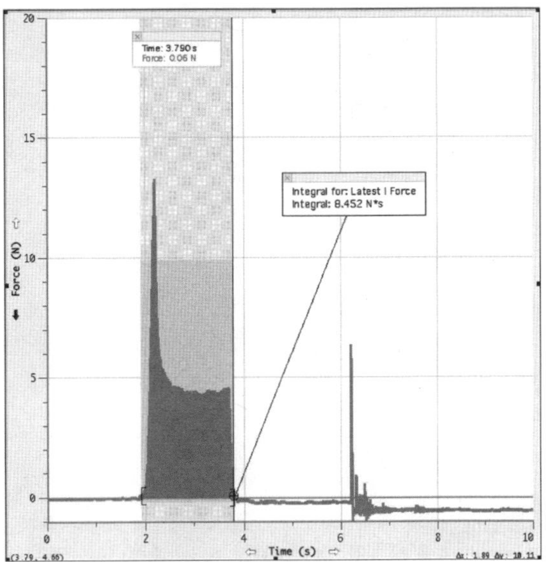

Conclusion

When using probeware, I prefer the computer as the microprocessor controlling the probes because it has a better screen resolution than either the calculator or the handheld device. The computer is usually able to collect the data at a faster sampling rate, which is useful in some investigations where the events in question are brief.

The characteristics of rapid data collection, nearly instantaneous display of data in tabular or graphical form, analysis tools, and the ability to collect data consistently over long periods of time enable probeware to be one of the most important tools at the science teacher's disposal. A new world of possible student investigations opens up with the use of these tools.

CHAPTER 5

Extending Inquiry With Geotechnologies in the Science Classroom

Thomas R. Baker

Geography has always played a pivotal role in the development of scientific thought. Alfred Russell Wallace (1885), recognizing the spatial proximities of related species, concluded that "Every species has come into existence closely coincident both in space and time with a pre-existing closely allied species," bringing to light one of the most basic phenomenon of nature, biologic evolution. Similarly, the identification of spatial clustering of disease outbreaks led John Snow to map and examine causal relationships (against popular medical opinion) that suggested a single water well in downtown London served as a point source for cholera. Snow's (1856) keen insight into the geographic relationships of people contracting cholera helped him formulate new ideas about the nature of disease and disease transmission.

Scientific data with a spatial component are critical for understanding a vast array of scientific and social issues, including species distribution, molecular modeling, urbanization models, geologic stratification, natural resource management, glacial retreat tracking, weather and climatology, global tectonic activity, and much more. Geotechnologies are tools that allow your students to learn the skills of collecting and analyzing data and creating representations of data with an emphasis on spatial relationships. These processes are critical in nearly every environmental and social investigation conducted in an inquiry-oriented classroom.

Geotechnologies (also called geospatial technologies) are hardware and software that use location-based data and analysis tools to accomplish tasks ranging from determining a location to creating dynamic models for visualizing real-time, map-based displays. Geotechnologies typically include Geographic Information Systems, the Global Positioning System, and remotely sensed data (e.g., aerial photography and satellite imagery). Other visualization technologies, including geographic animation, geographic data explorers, and immersive and stereoscopic displays, are also typically considered geotechnologies.

MORE ABOUT GIS

GIS systems can vary greatly in terms of cost and functionality. On the high end, professional grade GIS software commercially retails for thousands of dollars and requires substantial computing power that typically demands hardware upgrades to school computers. However, many of the leading GIS companies, such as ESRI, Inc. (*www.esri.com/k-12*) have K–12 programs and pricing that allow for the placement of these high-end tools in schools. Northwestern University's GEODE Initiative (*www.worldwatcher.northwestern.edu*) has also created a GIS specifically for K–12 students.

Geographic data explorers are commonly considered to be the younger sibling to a full-fledged GIS. These data explorers are free or low cost but have limited analytical functionality. Google Earth (*http://earth.google.com*) and ESRI's ArcGIS Explorer (*http://esri.com/arcexplorer*) are two geographic data explorer mainstays. Although all schools will find that using geographic data explorers are a good introductory step for integrating GIS into the curricula, schools with limited budgets will find that using data explorers also provides a flexible yet fascinating way for students to collect and view data.

Geographic Information Systems (GIS) are computer-based mapping programs designed for collecting, manipulating, and displaying data with a geographic component (such as latitude-longitude). A GIS organizes data into thematic layers. The concept is analogous to stacking multiple transparencies on an overhead projector to show how different information relates spatially. In a GIS, it is common to see a layer of roads, set atop a layer of hydrology, set atop a layer of vegetation. In this way, when you look at a GIS, the map of roads, hydrology, and vegetation all appear as a single map, yet the layers can be individually displayed or analyzed.

A GIS can also map more complex data, such as density and frequency of particular events (e.g., rates of disease outbreaks, occurrences of an invasive species, or locations of recent wildfires). A GIS can also perform geostatistics or correlations of data to a nearby area of interest. A GIS can even display real-time data, showing change over time or displaying data in an immersive or stereoscopic display.

The Global Positioning System (GPS) is a constellation of 24 satellites situated about 20,000 kilometers above Earth's surface. These satellite transmitters circle the earth every 12 hours, constantly producing timing signals that are received by handheld devices on or above the Earth's surface. When a handheld GPS receiver intercepts signals from at least three satellites, it trilaterates a latitude and longitude. Essentially, the GPS network gives every point on Earth a unique location identifier, much like an address. Oftentimes, a GPS receiver can plug into a laptop running a GIS to produce real-time maps. A more sophisticated GPS receiver may have maps with navigation and points of interest on board.

GPS receivers are becoming smaller all the time and embedded into other technologies, such as cell phones, cameras, watches, Personal Digital Assistants, automobiles, and boats. The price of a GPS receiver usually corresponds to its positional accuracy and extra functionality (like altimeters, maps, compass, etc). Retail stores around the United States provide base models for as little as $60 for a receiver. High-end, professional-grade receivers can cost tens of thousands of dollars.

Remote sensing (RS) is typically considered to be the gathering of electromagnetic energy, using a variety of satellite or aerial instruments and sensors. Although RS cameras and radars can create stunning imagery of our Earth, RS data can also be quantitatively analyzed using the raw numerical data, suitable for exploring nearly any area of interest, such as land use, geology, hydrology, vegetation, urbanization, and soils. In collecting imagery, different remote sensors are particularly well suited to gathering information about specific surfaces or phenomena, principally based upon the "bands" (identified portions of the electromagnetic spectrum) that are most informative. In terms of the geography, in a single pass, some remote sensors can collect information from areas as large as a continent or as focused as the garden in your backyard.

Since many of the RS satellites repeatedly monitor the same geographic area in a relatively short time frame, creating change-over-time mapping and analysis applications is common. With current and historical RS datasets, scientists can create models that predict annual vegetation growth, monitor change in species' habitats from human impacts, or estimate water quality based on changes in land use. Additionally, long-term RS data archives are now available online (e.g., Landsat imagery). Depending on the source and age of the RS data, price can vary greatly. For those schools with limited budgets or new to RS data, one approach is to use the free imagery available through geographic data explorers (see More About GIS, p. 44). This free imagery is downloaded into the geographic data viewers as it is needed, requiring less stringent computing resources.

What the Research Says

Geotechnologies in the science classroom are usually justified through one of three explanations: (a) support for spatial thinking, (b) support for workforce preparation, and (c) support for extending scientific inquiry.

The recent National Academies Press publication, *Learning to Think Spatially: GIS as a Support System in the K–12 Curriculum*, argues for the inclusion of spatial reasoning across the K–12 curriculum with special emphasis in geography and science. Spatial thinking, identified as the "cognitive tools… that allow for a constructive amalgam of three elements: concepts of space, tools of representation, and processes of reasoning," is integral to everyday life and too often neglected in the curriculum (NRC 2006). Improving spatial thinking is a primary reason schools should consider integrating GIS as a primary tool across the K–12 curriculum.

The need for technically skilled American workers in the field of geotechnologies has been underscored by the Department of Labor, citing the geotechnical industry as one of the three fastest-growing technology industries in America this decade. The geotechnical industry is expected to show at least a sixfold increase immediately and is identified by the Bush administration's "High-Growth Jobs Initiative." The first listed priority for the geotechnical industry by the DOL is, "expanding the pipeline of youth entering the geospatial technology industry." This bodes well for high school science instructors using geotechnologies to support and extend classroom inquiries, activities that increasingly mimic the field techniques of skilled professionals in science, technology, and engineering industries.

When geotechnologies are used as an instructional support in inquiry or problem-based learning, researchers have typically found improvements in both student attitude toward science and their ability to conduct scientific investigations (Kerski 2000; Olsen 2000). Improvements in student achievement can be seen in the accuracy of data analysis and the development of research conclusions within classroom scientific inquiry (Baker 2002; Crabb 2001). However, without prior instruction in map-based data manipulation and representation, the effects of geotechnologies appear to be dramatically reduced (Doering 2002).

GIS, specifically, can aid in identifying expert learner traits in problem-solving and navigational strategies (Wigglesworth 2000). Incorporating GIS into a curriculum has shown mixed research results for improving recall of content knowledge (Kerski 2000). Generally, the conclusions of researchers should not be surprising; the use of a suite of geographic data analysis technologies helps to extend the processes of scientific inquiry in the classroom.

Guidelines for Best Practice

Several recommendations can be garnered from educational research and development activities from the past 10 years of GIS in precollegiate education. Although the subsequent suggestions are intended for classrooms that use scientific inquiry or problem-based learning, they are equally appropriate to many instructional methodologies.

(1) Prepare students to use maps and spatial analysis tools effectively.

Basic map reading and interpretation can be difficult for students, particularly when using a GIS with several complex datasets. Prepare to explicitly teach map reading and analysis activities prior to expecting students to use map-based analyses as a part of an inquiry. Hang laminated vegetation, migratory, geology, or hydrol-

ogy maps on the classroom walls. Mark interesting or unique points on the map with transparency markers. Depending upon the GIS software you intend to use, a variety of materials are available to teach about GIS and map analysis. See the suggested reading list at the conclusion of this chapter for more information. Also consider having students find their home, school, and popular hangouts on a map or image of their hometown.

(2) Plan for a phased-in instructional approach when using GIS to support inquiry.

Based in part on Recommendation 1, using a GIS in a classroom requires planning and a patient, stepwise approach to successful integration. Instructionally, GIS is akin to a word processing or spreadsheet program, expecting the user to enter data and direct the GIS to "do" something with that data. Unlike a word processor or spreadsheet, the data available in a GIS can become staggeringly complicated due to data formats, projects, datums, accuracy issues, and the content of the data (e.g., What do these data mean? How accurate are these data? Why don't certain features align correctly?).

Use gradually increasing GIS technology, map interpretation, and inquiry skills in a progressive framework, such as the one used by the NSF-funded *Extending Scientific Inquiry Through G.I.S.* program (NSF #0096679). The framework increases the complexity of technology use and application to inquiry by first presenting maps and data to students through creating data and multidimensional visualizations:

- **Presentation:** You or your students show maps from a science textbook or website to an audience. The audience does not interact with the map, but views the information and context selected by the map presenter.
- **Exploration:** The task of exploration is one of data discovery, investigation, and searching. At this point, students start to "fool around" with GIS software and data. Students may turn data layers on and off, make layers active, or even add/delete existing data layers in a GIS or data explorer. Exploration is a stage where students can view immediately available data layers and simply see what's there. For example, students may use a geographic data explorer to see in what watershed their school lies as a precursor to a water quality study. Similarly, students might use websites (e.g., the MapMachine at *http://nationalgeographic.com/mapmachine*) to study conservation and historical hurricane maps.
- **Analysis:** In the analysis phase, data layers are compared and contrasted against one another. In some cases, data are identified based upon relationships with other data. Analysis tasks could include identifying what's inside, outside, or nearby another object or class of objects. For example,

students working collaboratively might study phenology using GIS to gather and spatially analyze the variables identified in Hopkin's Law of Bioclimatics (elevation, latitude, and longitude) in addition to other suspect variables such as temperature, moisture, and light. Students collect their own indicators of spring (i.e., frog calls, cricket sounds, first dandelion) and create a GIS project in which each data layer can be examined for spatial correlation with student-collected indicators of spring, confirming or extending Hopkin's Law.

- **Synthesis:** Creating new data layers and/or recombining existing data layers into new, previously unknown patterns is the hallmark of synthesis. Students take the knowledge they have previously learned about science and GIS use and apply the knowledge to a new, unknown situation. For example, students may create a single new layer from three of the environmental factors listed in the analysis phase (e.g., elevation, precipitation, and temperature), in an attempt to create a single composite data layer. The single, new data layer can then be used to assess student-collected data.
- **Visualization:** Visualization is the process of searching for new patterns within the data layers and includes the manipulation of the way map data are represented. Alterations of the classification (including color palette and legend types) or map styles are considered potential visualization approaches. More recently, three- and four-dimensional modeling, animations, and stereoscopic displays have been considered among the foremost efforts to create geographic visualizations.

(3) Guide students through inquiries that are local in focus and bring in collaborators. Inquiry investigations that have deep roots in students' communities elevate motivation through a sense of ownership in the problem and solution. For many Earth science and environmental investigations, a personal knowledge of the geographic area is critical to the success of the study. Data collection technologies, like a GPS receiver, are naturally best suited to local investigations, but so is the use of GIS. Not only are you more likely to have a greater volume of local data at your disposal, the data is also more likely to be current.

Although substantial amounts of data can be freely downloaded from commercial and governmental websites, a far more expansive array of data most likely sits in your county's mapping or GIS office. Establish and nurture an ongoing relationship with professionals in that office. Often, you'll find that your local county mapping office can provide data, create poster-size prints of maps, and even provide some degree of technical support. An excellent opportunity to establish this relationship is by calling your county's mapping office and inviting a GIS analyst to speak to your class on GIS Day, an annual event occurring in mid-November.

(4) Scale the technology with your personal comfort level and the school's technical capacity.

Geotechnologies, particularly GIS, are available to classrooms at a variety of levels:

- Step 1: For those new to GIS, creating maps with a desktop GIS or map-making website and then incorporating those images into presentation software is a good first step for creating presentations. In this way, the use of GIS can facilitate many different instructional strategies, including scientific inquiry.

- Step 2: Moving students into internet-based mapping is often the next step in the technical progression. Internet-based mapping sites are becoming increasingly common and increasingly more powerful as tools for exploring map data—a good approach to supporting the collection of background information for an inquiry.

- Step 3: The third step usually involves downloading and installing a free GIS data viewer to school computers. ESRI's ArcExplorer for Education or Google Earth are geographic data viewers that allow for importing a variety of data with some cartographic or mathematical analysis tools. Many of these free viewers also give students their first opportunity to incorporate data they have collected with a GPS and satellite imagery they have downloaded from the internet.

- Step 4: The fourth step is often purchasing and installing a full-fledged GIS. In recent years, Northwestern's MyWorld, ESRI's ArcView, and Intergraph's Geomedia have become increasingly popular in schools. These applications support the widest variety of GIS, RS, and GPS data while supporting a wide array of analysis tools. The potential payoff for using these more robust GIS applications is the facilitation of school-to-career paths for students and better compatibility with collaborators, such as your county mapping office.

Examples of Best Practice

A variety of examples can be found where this integrative suite of technology blends physical, Earth, and biological sciences within inquiry. The examples that follow illustrate a few common cases for geotechnology inclusion in the secondary science class.

Water Quality

In Kansas, where water quality and quantity are politically sensitive issues, students at a local high school travel to a nearby stream, measuring chemical, biological, visual, and location information. The collected data is returned to the classroom, where student teams map and study their results using a GIS with supporting data from the county mapping office (including hydrology, soils, vegetation, and land-use data). Later in the school year, the students will use previous GPS receiver readings to locate the exact location of their previous data collections, so that they can document and study seasonal changes in water quality. By using standardized collection and analysis protocols, the students are subsequently able to share and discuss their water quality data with other schools in the county.

Ecological Patterns

The study of Wisconsin's wildlife and natural resources takes a cutting edge when students use GIS, GPS, and RS data to explore original research questions about ecology. The Wildlands Science Research School near Augusta works closely with state and county agencies and has been able to track, map, and predict ecological patterns in several plant and animal species. Among the results, student efforts have assisted in re-evaluating and further extending the implementation of the state's natural resource management plan.

Students' Home Ranges

As an introductory study in biology, students establish their personal home ranges by carrying a GPS receiver on their person after school and on weekends for a week. Each student's GPS receiver automatically logs their position every 10 minutes, data that is periodically downloaded to disk and brought to class. The student-collected data is displayed in a GIS at point locations, which are then converted into density maps, with the darkest areas of the map indicating geographic areas most popular with the student. Small groups, classes, or multiple classes can then share and/or combine their data to establish aggregated maps. Street networks, zoning and parcel data, and high-resolution aerial photography can be incorporated to provide greater meaning to the data. In effect, the exercise establishes a student's (or group's) home-range boundary. Concepts such as carrying capacity, habitat, and migratory studies in a biology or health class are then linked into the students' home range studies.

A Local Natural Heritage Inventory

In Vermont, students began recording the location of vegetation plots and species with a GIS and GPS receiver, establishing a map of the surrounding environment on land owned (or under agreement) by the high school. Essentially creating a local natural heritage inventory, students were able to document the location (or presence and absence) of several animal species, taking careful field notes and digital photos. The data were then placed into a GIS, including photos and notes that were hyperlinked to web pages on the school's server. Moreover, the students were able to incorporate color aerial photography into the GIS, to better understand how the school property and the surrounding land have changed over the past several years.

Relative Air Quality

Earth science students studying atmospheric conditions began using lichens as bioindicators of relative air quality, where the density and diversity of lichen species (and even morphology) is correlated to quantity of atmospheric sulphur dioxide (SO_2). Using a GPS receiver, students locate a tree of prespecified species and standardized measurement grid to calculate a lichen index. The latitude, longitude, tree species, and lichen index are uploaded into an internet database. Students can then retrieve spreadsheets and maps of their data and their peers' data, as they look for mathematical and spatial patterns in lichen density and diversity. Through text and spatial queries, students work directly with the map data, creating maps filtered on several variables and overlaid with other relevant thematic data (e.g., land use, vegetation indices, and urbanization). The internet-based GIS technology allows a level of exploration, analysis, and peer collaboration typically out of reach for introductory students.

Conclusion

Geotechnologies are a spatial data collection, analysis, and visualization tool kit. For most, the implementation of one or more of these technologies will be implemented progressively, catering the use of technology to your comfort level and increasing the technology integration and shifting instructional practices as your needs change. To help ease the way into advanced uses of geotechnologies, consider a *Presentation→ Exploration→Analysis→Synthesis→Visualization* approach. In the early stages of your work with geotechnology, find local collaborators, GIS analysts, and other teachers using GIS to call on for support. Join some of the GIS educator networks on the web, such as KanGIS (*http://kangis.org*) or EdGIS (*https://list.terc.edu/mailman/listinfo/edgis*) to keep abreast of new data sources, training workshops, and software.

If you prefer using prepared materials in the classroom, conduct searches for GIS lessons on the web. Many of these resources are high quality and provide data and a teacher guide in a single downloadable package. Although a variety of suitable materials for teaching about GIS exist, there are relatively few materials for inquiry-based teaching of secondary science with GIS. When deciding whether to use GIS, allow your instructional and content needs to instigate and direct your use of geotechnology, rather than using these technologies to dictate your instructional and content needs. After all, as science educators, we teach *with* geotechnology and not necessarily *about* geotechnology.

Suggested Readings

Audet, R. H., and G. Ludwig, eds. 2000. *GIS in schools*. Redlands, CA: ESRI Press.

Downs, R., and A. deSouza, eds. 2006. *Learning to think spatially: GIS as a support system in the K–12 curriculum*. Washington, DC: National Academy Press.

Green, D. R., Ed. 2001. *GIS: A sourcebook for schools*. London: Taylor and Francis.

Malone, L., A. M. Palmer, and C. L. Voigt. 2002. *Mapping our world: GIS lessons for educators*. Redlands, CA: ESRI Press.

Mitchell, A. 1999. *The ESRI guide to spatial analysis volume 1: Geographic patterns and relationships*. Redlands, CA: ESRI Press.

Acquiring Online Data for Scientific Analysis

Kathy Cabe Trundle

Scientific inquiry, a component of scientific literacy targeted in the National Science Education Standards, allows us to explore nature and propose explanations based on evidence. The Standards define scientific inquiry as "a set of interrelated processes by which scientists and students pose questions about the natural world and investigate phenomena" (NRC 1996, p. 214). Inquiry includes posing questions, planning and conducting investigations, using tools to gather and analyze data, formulating data-based explanations, representing data, and communicating findings (see also *Science as Inquiry in the Secondary Setting,* by Luft, Bell, and Gess-Newsome).

As you seek to provide more opportunities for your students to engage in scientific inquiry, however, you may find data collection to be time consuming and expensive. The internet, which provides immediate access to numerous data sets from government agencies, global corporations, colleges and universities, and other institutions, can provide a solution.

The internet allows students to access existing data sets and explore phenomena beyond their classroom and school settings, like tracking migratory routes and identifying breeding areas of water birds in South Africa. Online data sets extend the possibilities of inquiry beyond the limitations and constraints of available equipment and geographic locations.

As researchers have increased their use of the internet for the dissemination of research results, many also have placed primary data sets online. Although the original intent probably was to make data available to other researchers, teachers can incorporate these free and easily accessible resources into their classroom instruction. Online data generally can be grouped into two broad categories, existing data sets and data collected collaboratively, like the GLOBE (Global Learning and Observations to Benefit the Environment) Program.

Data sets are available as raw data in spreadsheets, text files, aerial and satellite images, maps, and graphs. For example, the U.S. Geological Survey (USGS) website provides data on earthquakes, volcanic activity, and water quality. From this website, teachers can access data on arsenic in the 31,350 ground-water samples collected in 1973–2001 by the USGS, available in spreadsheets or text files and including the state and site where the water sample was collected, the date and time of collection, the latitude and longitude of the well, the primary use of the water, and the depth of the well. Teachers can use this data set to have students plot the arsenic levels in their area and compare them to neighboring counties and states.

Figure 1.

U.S. Geological Survey Geology home page.

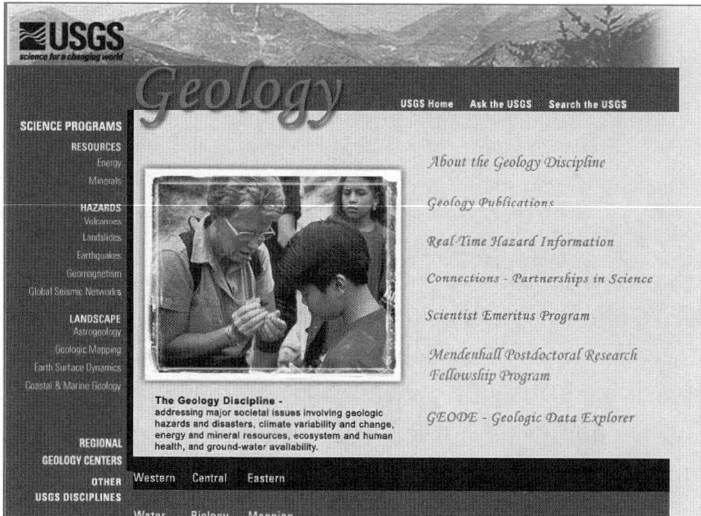

What the Research Says

Research findings indicate that using online data in inquiry-based instruction has many potential benefits, including gains in students' content knowledge and increases in student interest, engagement, motivation, and sense of control of learning.

A number of researchers have found that using online data to address authentic problems resulted in increased student motivation (Lenk 1992; Means and Olson 1995; Mistler-Jackson and Songer 2000; Songer 1996, 1998). The researchers attributed the increase in motivation to students viewing the learning experience as worthwhile and meaningful.

Windschitl (1998) found that the ability to access data on a wide range of topics can support inquiry by prompting student-generated inquiry questions. Since the available information is so diverse, students are likely to find topics aligned with their individual interests, which can spark interest and make the inquiry more personally relevant.

Other research has found that using the internet to access data about current events makes students feel empowered with their use of inquiry skills (Lenk 1992; Songer 1996, 1998), and students demonstrated statistically significant improvements in science content and inquiry skills (Mistler-Jackson and Songer 2000; Songer 1998;

Songer, Lee, and Kam 2002). For example, in two studies with inner-city students (Lee and Songer 2003; Songer, Lee, and Kam 2002), researchers studied students who were involved in a real-time weather forecasting project in which the students gathered and analyzed data from the internet on fronts and pressure systems. The results indicated that students (including students who were typically the lowest performing) increased their science content knowledge and improved their inquiry performance.

Some research has examined networked science projects in which students, teachers, or scientists shared online data and collaborated about shared problems or current events. An example of this type of project is the GLOBE Program. Findings from the research on these types of projects indicated an increase in student interest and accountability, an increase in student engagement (including by students who were not usually interested or successful in science), and a decrease in absenteeism during the projects (Lenk 1992; Songer 1996, 1998).

Guidelines for Best Practice

Although using online data in inquiry-based lessons is a fairly new field, a synthesis of the work of the teachers and researchers who have explored this area yields some helpful guidelines to make the practice easier and more effective.

(1) Limit student searches to targeted websites and simplified data sets.

The volume of accessible data can be overwhelming for teachers and students, and real data sets can be messy. Also, some principals and school administrators may limit student access to the internet out of fear that students may access inappropriate material such as pornography. To address these issues teachers can copy and paste URLs into a word processing document or develop class or subject homepages that contain links to specific websites (Lynch and Walton 1998). Teachers can also use web pages that are configured without search capabilities, or they can capture all targeted pages and create an off-line browsing site on the school's computer. One easy way to develop a web page for student use is through the online system TrackStar (*http://trackstar.4teachers.org/trackstar*), which allows you to collect URLs, enter them into the TrackStar system, and add annotations for your students.

(2) Make the learning relevant.

You can integrate data into authentic tasks that address problems faced by scientists, such as mapping earthquake activity, forecasting the weather, or monitoring air quality (Hunter and Xie 2001; Means and Olson 1995; Slater and Fixen 1998). Also, you can use data from the school community to increase student interest in the project. According to Lee and Songer (2003) authentic problems use real-world problems faced by scientists, have students seek solutions to problems in their own lives, and/or link students and scientists through data sharing. Authentic tasks or problems help students see an activity as being worthwhile and meaningful. By making assignments relevant, students who are not typically interested in science may find science learning more engaging. Finally, using online data sources facilitates teaching students about multicultural aspects of science by exposing them to the efforts of researchers from other countries.

(3) Integrate data into inquiry that reflect the science process.
The National Science Education Standards call for teaching science concepts through scientific inquiry. Inquiry includes identifying important questions, observing, recording data, classifying, looking for patterns, analyzing data, verifying results, and communicating findings to others. To help students develop their inquiry skills, Windschitl (1998) recommended the following for use with online data:

- **Develop questions:** Help students understand what constitutes an inquiry-based question and frame a driving investigative question around the data. Often students are not skilled at asking questions that can be answered with data. Teachers and students must work together to develop appropriate questions and allow students to reframe their questions if the data indicate their questions are unclear or inappropriate.

- **Analyze data:** Allow students to develop their own strategies for analyzing data and interpreting evidence. Provide a scaffold for working with outliers in the data.

- **Communicate findings:** Emphasize the role of argument to support claims or assertions, and engage students in discussions about the validity of their findings.

(4) Contact education centers to request help.
Many teachers may not have the time to filter the large volume of existing data for the most usable subsets. Many of the organizations that generate and store data also have an educational resource person on staff to work with teachers. Teachers who wish to use online data may contact the centers to request help in meeting their instructional needs (Lynch and Walton 1998).

Examples of Best Practice

Science educators recommend incorporating web-based data into inquiry activities, and many such activities have been published. Online data are available in all areas of science (e.g., life, physical, and Earth and space science) and in various formats. Examples for each content area follow.

Earth and Space Science

In Earth and space science, students can discover tidal patterns by using online data sources and spreadsheets for data analysis. They can import data into spreadsheets, cull data, calculate daily tidal ranges, create and interpret line graphs of tides and tidal ranges, correlate Moon phase data with tidal range data, and describe relationships between phenomena. (See Tidal Data below for more specific details about this activity.)

TIDAL DATA

In a class of ninth-grade Earth science students, a colleague and I limited students' access to data to one site, the Center for Operational Oceanographic Products and Services, Verified/Historic (Tides) Water Level Data retrieval page (*http://tidesandcurrents.noaa.gov/station_retrieve.shtml?type=Tide+Data*). We also initially limited the geographic location to one place, FPF Pier, in Duck, North Carolina, and to the same time period so that all students were using the same data set. This gave all students the same initial point of reference and comparison for additional analyses. Also, we were better able to quickly identify any problems when a student's graph did not fit the expected pattern.

To make the learning relevant, we asked students to select another time period for the same geographic location, and many students selected their birthdates. We also asked students to select a different geographic location to compare to the analysis for Duck, North Carolina. Many students selected coastal locations where their families had vacationed or areas near where extended family members lived.

Students used data and modeling to answer the question "What causes tides?" Through their work, students were interested to see what happened in these areas during hurricane seasons, and they also came up with additional questions such as, "How do tides compare during different seasons?"

Students were provided a model for importing data into a spreadsheet and for analyzing and representing the data in graphs. However, students were encouraged to think of subsequent questions and come up with their own strategies for analyzing data to answer their questions.

Students looked for anomalies in the patterns in their data. For example, some students found an extreme peak in their tidal range that did not correspond with springtides. The students inferred that a storm could have caused the extreme fluctuation in the tidal range. Using the internet, the students looked at newspaper reports from the targeted areas and found that a hurricane had struck during the time period in question.

Other data that may be used in Earth and space science include earthquake and volcano data related to plate boundaries, latitude and longitude of specific cities to access plate motion data and calculate the directions and rates of plate movements, temperature data from different geographic locations to describe climates and climate changes, hurricane impacts on landforms and geographic features, oceanography (e.g., sea floor spreading), river patterns, and volcanic ash and weather patterns.

Some websites that provide data for Earth and space science lessons include the following:

- **Science in Your Backyard, U.S. Geological Survey:** State-specific water data, streamflow, floods and high water data, groundwater levels, earthquake activity. *www.usgs.gov/state*

Figure 2.

The USGS "Science In Your Backyard" web page.

Select a location from the map below or select from a list.

- **National Oceanic and Atmospheric Administration, Center for Operational Oceanographic Products and Services:** Verified/historic (Tides) Water Level Data retrieval page. *http://tidesandcurrents.noaa.gov/station_retrieve.shtml?type=Tide+Data*

- **Plate Motion Calculator, UNAVCO:** Calculate tectonic plate motion at any location on Earth. *http://sps.unavco.org/crustal_motion/dxdt/nnrcalc*

- **Surfing for Earthquakes and Volcanoes (Coe and Merrick, UC Berkeley):** Earthquake and volcano data with lessons. *http://cse.ssl.berkeley.edu/lessons/indiv/coe/details.html*

- **EPA Envirofacts Data Warehouse, U.S. Environmental Protection Agency:** A national information system that provides an integrated single point of access to data extracted from six major EPA databases.
  www.epa.gov/enviro

- **Air Quality System Database, U.S. Environmental Protection Agency:** Database contains measurements of air pollutant concentrations in the 50 states.
  www.epa.gov/air/data/aqsdb.html

- **Search Your Community, U.S. Environmental Protection Agency:** Get specific environmental information about your neighborhood by entering your zip code on this site.
  www.epa.gov/epahome/commsearch.htm

Physical Science

Students also can access and use data in physical science classes. They can use an interactive periodic table (*www.chemicool.com*) to access data about different elements, including atomic radii, electronegativity, and first ionization energy to describe periodic trends and explain the organizational principles for the periodic table. Students can use sports speed records to plot record speeds over time and infer explanations for speed trends. Also, most teenagers are interested in driving and cars. Students can access automobile performance test data to calculate time, velocity, and mass for the accelerating automobile. They can calculate kinetic energy versus time data and graph it, and they can graph time versus speed.

Some websites that provide data for Physical Science lessons include the following:

- **ChemiCool Periodic Table:**
  www.chemicool.com

- **USA Rollersports Speed Skating Records:**
  www.usarollersports.org/vnews/display.v/ART/40046cf801d44

- **International Skiing History Association World Speed Skiing Records 1874–1999:**
  http://skiinghistory.org/Speed.html

- **Physics Factbook—Speed of the Fastest Human, Running:**
  http://hypertextbook.com/facts/2000/KatarzynaJanuszkiewicz.shtml

- **Road Test Data—Automobile Magazine:**
  www.caranddriver.com/newreviewsroad

Life Science

In life science, students can identify migratory routes and breeding areas for various animals, including sea turtles, water birds, great apes, and arctic animals. They can access data about different animals' migratory routes and/or breeding areas, plot the data onto maps, and compare the data for different time periods to see how the patterns have changed over time.

Other life science topics include analyzing global tap water, human population trends, human census data over time, types and amounts of marine debris, and water monitoring.

Some websites that provide data for life science lessons include the following:

- **U.S. Geological Survey—Water use in the United States:** 50 years of data.
  http://water.usgs.gov/watuse

- **U.S. Geological Survey—National Water Quality Assessment Data Warehouse:** Chemical, biological, and physical water quality data from 42 basins across the nation.
  http://infotrek.er.usgs.gov/traverse/f?p=NAWQA:HOME:4072984908919821

- **National Oceanic and Atmospheric Administration National Ocean Service:** Includes data on coral reef conservation, coastal ecosystem science, natural hazards assessment, and oil and chemical spills.
  http://oceanservice.noaa.gov/dataexplorer/data_topics/welcome.html

- **Marine Turtle Interactive Mapping System, UNEP World Conservation Monitoring Centre:**
  http://stort.unep-wcmc.org/imaps/indturtles/viewer.htm

- **Great Apes Survival Project, UNEP World Conservation Monitoring:**
  http://stort.unep-wcmc.org/imaps/grasp/viewer.htm

- **Migratory Waterbirds, African Eurasian Migratory Waterbird Agreement, UNEP World Conservation Monitoring:**
  http://stort.unepwcmc.org/imaps/AEWA/viewer.htm?Title=AEWA

- **World Atlas of Biodiversity, UNEP World Conservation Monitoring:**
  http://stort.unep-wcmc.org/imaps/gb2002/book/viewer.htm

- **U.S. Census Bureau Lessons Using Census 2000 Data:** *www.census.gov/dmd/www/schoolessons.html*

- **U.S. Geological Survey: Wandering Wildlife:** Satellite and Radio Telemetry Tracking Wildlife Across the Arctic: Includes polar bears, loons, sockeye salmon, brant, common eider, and long-tailed ducks. *http://alaska.usgs.gov/science/biology/wandering_wildlife*

- **National Cancer Institute, State Cancer Profiles:** Dynamic views of cancer statistics. *http://statecancerprofiles.cancer.gov*

Figure 3.

"Wandering Wildlife" web page.

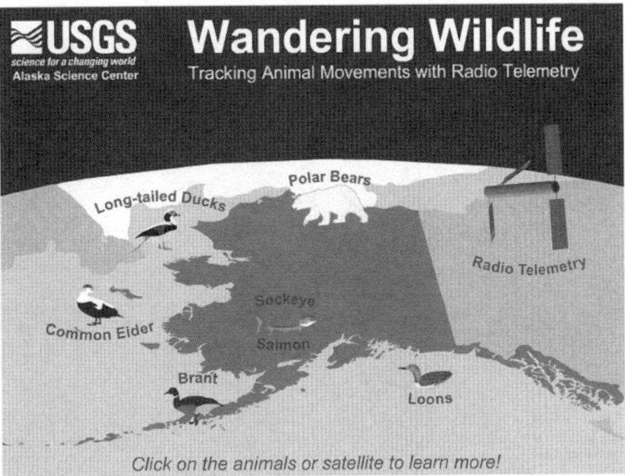

In addition to the websites that provide access to data, several resources are available that offer lesson plans and instructional ideas about how to access data through the internet. One example is the Network Montana Project, a site funded by the National Science Foundation that offers instructional materials on the atmosphere, geosphere, hydrosphere, and mountain environments (Slater and Beaudrie 1998). The website can be accessed at *www.math.montana.edu/~nmp*.

Conclusion

By using online data, students can ask questions about scientific phenomena and develop methods for answering their questions. They can collect data by accessing existing data sets and they can organize their data. They can use the data to make inferences, they can represent their data in graphs, and they can communicate the findings to their teachers and classmates. By integrating online data into inquiry-based lessons, teachers can help students develop their inquiry skills as they develop their science content knowledge. As an added bonus, students also will develop important technology skills as they use online databases to import data sets into spreadsheets, construct data tables, make graphs, and produce presentations.

CHAPTER 7

Web-Based Science Inquiry Projects

Alec M. Bodzin

Student groups in Juanita Jones' science classroom are investigating marine mammal migration patterns. Each group examines web-based archived migration data sets of different species that have had satellite tags placed on them. The elephant seal group notes that their seals travel 3,000 miles and arrive on a California shore at two different times during the year. In addition, they observe that both males and females arrive at the same location in the winter, but return to the same place at different times during the year. Students make inferences about the purposes of their visits to shore and raise new questions. They then consider scientists' research concerning the seals' migration. Finally, they communicate their findings to their classmates with a PowerPoint presentation that highlights the different migration patterns of male and female elephant seals.

This vignette illustrates a web-based inquiry (WBI) learning activity. Such activities support students as active learners. In these activities, students do not wait for a teacher or someone else to provide an answer. They conduct investigations with meaningful questions about everyday experiences, evaluate evidence critically to seek solutions, and ask new questions. Such inquiry-based approaches allow students to learn scientific practices by using those practices realistically. Learners who experience inquiry-based activities and instructional methods develop a broad understanding of science, along with the critical reasoning and problem-solving skills involved in scientific reasoning.

The web can be used to support inquiry learning in many classroom science investigations; however, not all web-based science activities are inquiry-learning activities. In fact, the majority of science activities on the web are designed to provide learners with scientific facts and concepts and do not engage learners with using scientific processes.

Web-based inquiry (WBI) projects are based on *Inquiry and the National Science Education Standards'* (NRC 2000) five "essential features" of scientific inquiry:

- Pursuing a scientifically oriented question.
- Collecting evidence related to that question.
- Drawing conclusions based on that evidence.
- Considering alternative conclusions.
- Communicating and justifying conclusions.

WBI projects require learners to use evidence and practices of the same type actual scientists use. Further, their activities emphasize reasoning and critical discussions of conclusions. Such inquiries may be *standalone* or *teacher facilitated* and may call for a combination of online and in-class activities. These projects combine group and individual work as appropriate. The extent to which the teacher directs or facilitates varies according to the nature of the inquiry. You can use the criteria listed in Table 1 to help you evaluate the characteristics of WBI activities.

Table 1.

Criteria for Evaluating a Web-Based Inquiry (WBI) Activity.

Characteristics	Criteria
Three Inquiry Essentials	Does the WBI contain at least the first three essential features of classroom inquiry described in *Inquiry and the National Science Education Standards* (NRC 2000)?
	Learners are engaged by scientifically oriented questions that are stated explicitly or implied as a task.
	Learners give priority to evidence, which allows them to draw conclusions and/or develop and evaluate explanations that address scientifically oriented questions.
	Learners draw conclusions and/or formulate explanations from evidence to address scientifically oriented questions.
Learner Centered	Is the WBI phrased in such a way that learners would perceive it as directed at them? In a learner center project, the majority of the wording used in the WBI is directed at the learner ("you"), not at the teacher ("your students").
Student Learning Science Concept or Content	Does the project support student learning of a science concept or science content? Science WBIs should fall into a recognized science discipline (biology, chemistry, physics, environmental sciences, astronomy, oceanography, and the like).
Web-Based	Is the WBI web-based? A WBI should be more than reformatted text from printed sheets placed on the web, describing how an inquiry activity may be completed. Instead, it should be enhanced or customized to take advantage of the features of the web to deliver instruction.

Scientific Evidence	Is the evidence used in the WBI of the same type an actual scientist would use?
Conclusions or Explanations Involve Reasoning	Are the conclusions and explanations in the WBI more than simple data analysis and reporting? They should involve reasoning.

Most WBIs are developed by science educators at universities, government agencies, and informal science education organizations and often take advantage of a variety of technology-based instructional resources that textbooks and other print materials are unable to offer (Bodzin and Cates 2002). Only a desktop computer containing a web browser (such as Internet Explorer, Safari, or Netscape) and an internet connection is needed.

Communication

Communication is an important feature of web-based inquiry projects. In an inquiry, the intent of communication is to share explanations and conclusions in order to permit one's fellow scientists to "ask questions, examine evidence, identify faulty reasoning, point out statements that go beyond the evidence, and suggest alternative explanations for the same observations" (NRC 2000, p. 27). Communication involves sharing with an audience other than the teacher. In a WBI activity, an audience might consist of fellow students, other users of the website, the website's developer(s), or a scientist.

There are three main types of science inquiry projects on the web:

- Comprehensive websites
- Collaborative projects
- Curricular enhancement activities

Types of WBI

Comprehensive Websites: Comprehensive websites are usually large websites that include both curricular activities and web-based resources to support an in-depth study of a particular science topic or geographical area. These sites contain instructional materials that meet all WBI criteria and often include scientific data or other materials that constitute "evidence" for an investigation. In addition, comprehensive websites contain important background knowledge that learners may need to understand to complete an inquiry. The WhaleNet website (*http://whale.wheelock.edu*) at Wheelock College is an example of a comprehensive site that provides extensive marine mammal background information and WBI activities that use authentic data sets to study marine mammal migration patterns.

Collaborative Projects: Collaborative projects involve learners from diverse geographical locations using a shared database to complete an investigation. In these investigations, evidence is used in two distinct ways. First, learners are provided with a protocol to collect certain data. Once collected, these data are submitted to a collective database. Next, the website provides learners with cumulative data from diverse geographical locations and prompts learners to analyze the cumulative data. In many collaborative projects, the host website also provides a discussion area for students to share thoughts and report conclusions. The Annenberg Media's Journey North Monarch Butterfly website (*www.learner.org/jnorth/monarch*) is an example of a collaborative project that permits learners to investigate the monarch butterfly annual migration through North America.

Curricular Enhancement Activities: Curricular enhancement activities are topic-oriented investigations designed to augment one's science curriculum. These activities are designed to be applicable to a wide range of audiences. Typically, the length of these activities may vary from one day to two weeks. Projects may take a variety of forms. For example, students may develop solutions to problems such as designing a bridge that can endure an earthquake, or they might investigate a critical habitat in a wetland and prepare a report to persuade others of the value of protecting that site. The *Earth Exploration Toolbook* (EET) chapter, "When is Dinner Served? Predicting the Spring Phytoplankton Bloom in the Gulf of Maine" (*http://serc.carleton.edu/eet/phytoplankton*) is an example of a curricular enhancement activity, in which learners investigate the timing of the spring phytoplankton bloom in the Gulf of Maine and predict where the bloom should occur.

What the Research Says

Online inquiry projects began with the idea of creating communication links among classrooms to share e-mail and data. In 1986, a series of projects was created to link classrooms through telecommunications to become a global school community. These projects, such as the National Geographic Society Kids Network (TERC 1986), were designed for students to investigate authentic problems that were not yet solved by scientists. They would collect and submit data to a centralized community database, make interpretations of the data, share thoughts and ideas across the network, and elaborate on the ideas put forth by others.

In the early 1990s, TERC and other science education groups created a group of subsequent "network science" projects. These included Global Lab (TERC), Kids as Global Scientists (University of Michigan), Classroom BirdWatch (Cornell Lab of Ornithology), and EstuaryNet (Wells Estuarine Reserve, Maine). These pioneering projects promoted important features of inquiry-based instruction and took advantage of computers with Internet connections for use in schools. Successful teacher participation in these complex and demanding curricular projects required a great deal of expertise in a diverse set of areas, including time management and inquiry-based teaching approaches (Songer 1998).

Research findings from these "network science" projects have noted that the design of the curricular activities and the nature of support provided for these projects plays an important role in promoting student understandings (Feldman et al. 2000; Songer 1998). In these projects, the use of real-time internet resources and using collaborating students as information resources for data reporting has the potential to enhance student understandings of scientific phenomena. For example, the peer-to-peer dialogue of students in the Kids as Global Scientists project included explanations and information about scientific information (Songer 1996). However, researchers also contended that, when collaborative projects do not design materials to promote reflective discourse that engages students in critical discussions about their data, the student dialogue may tend to be more social in nature and not related to the scientific investigation being studied (Feldman et al. 2000).

Web-based science curricular enhancement activities were being developed in the mid-1990s by university, informal science educators, and corporate partnerships with schools. By the late 1990s, science education website developers began establishing large comprehensive websites that included both web-based resources and curricular activities. Information about select science inquiry projects on the web is provided in the box on the following page.

Guidelines for Best Practice

Like most curricular activities, WBIs do not accommodate every learner, classroom teacher's pedagogical style, or classroom-learning environment. The following design guidelines modified from the Synergy Communities Aggregating Learning About Education (SCALE; *http://scale.soe.berkeley.edu*) curricular framework describe a helpful way for using a web-based science inquiry project (Bodzin and Shive 2004):

(1) Provide a motivating entry point.

Provide an activity or story to introduce the project and motivate student interest (e.g., an introduction to a locally relevant problem or a fictional story). The project should begin with phenomena that students find interesting. The focus of the investigation should be local. For example, if conducting an investigation to compare ponds in the United States, show digital photos of a nearby pond that has been used as a trash disposal area to illustrate a local environmental problem. Provide students with opportunities through class discussion to demonstrate that they understand the issue and what they might need to do to address it. Include background information about the problem or about the physical setting if needed.

SELECT SCIENCE INQUIRY PROJECTS ON THE WEB

Comprehensive sites

GLOBE (Global Learning and Observations to Benefit the Environment): The GLOBE program is implemented through a cooperative agreement between NASA, the University Corporation for Atmospheric Research (UCAR) in Boulder, Colorado, and Colorado State University in Fort Collins, Colorado. The GLOBE program supports a worldwide network of students who make environmental observations. Data is submitted and used for the developing scientific data visualizations. The site includes many inquiry-based learning activities.
(www.globe.gov)

Water on the Web: This extensive website for lake and stream water quality investigations resides at the University of Minnesota. Data is provided in real-time and archived formats from Remote Underwater Sampling Stations and stream monitoring stations located in Minnesota, as well as from cooperating projects nationwide. Data visualization tools enable students to watch data change through time, and view several parameters simultaneously.
(http://waterontheweb.org)

Collaborative Projects

Pathfinder Science: This project was established in 1997 with support from a U.S. Department of Education Technology Innovation Challenge grant as the Kansas Collaborative Research Network. Activities use a guided research inquiry framework for environmental and biological science investigations. The website includes protocols, data submission, retrieval from interactive databases, background information for research areas, and a publication area for students to submit and display their research work.
(http://pathfinderscience.net)

Classroom FeederWatch: Developed and located at the Cornell Lab of Ornithology, this project was once known as Classroom BirdWatch. Students construct bird feeders and conduct a winter survey of the birds that visit feeders in North America. The collected data is used each year by ornithologists to track changes in the abundance and distribution of bird species that use feeders in winter.
(www.birds.cornell.edu/cfw)

CEISE Collaborative Projects: This website is developed by the Stevens Institute of Technology's Center for Innovation in Engineering and Science Education. The site houses a series of collaborative projects in a variety of science topics. Student-collected data is contributed to a shared, web database. Activities involve student publishing on the web.
(www.k12science.org/collabprojs.html)

Curricular Enhancement Activities

Project Athena, Earth and Space Science for K–12: This site was developed in partnership by Science Applications International Corporation and the Office of Superintendent of Public Instruction in the state of Washington. This site includes curricular activities for the study of oceans, Earth resources, weather, space, and astronomy. (*http://vathena.arc.nasa.gov*).

WISE—Web-based Inquiry Science Environment: This website from the University of California, Berkeley contains a variety of secondary science projects in life, Earth, and physical science topic areas. Projects are interdisciplinary and primarily focus on real-world application of science-process skills. (*http://wise.berkeley.edu*).

(2) Provide access to authentic data.
Provide students with opportunities to explore authentic data. Data may originate from students' own data collection, historical data, a simplified data set, or elsewhere. The data should be authentic, come from a reputable source and relate directly to the problem at hand.

(3) Provide students with the means to make sense of the data.
Provide students with access to materials and activities that help them to understand and interpret the data. This includes making sure important background information is included and tools are provided that help students organize data and identify patterns. Data sets need to be simple in design. Real data tends to be messy, and large data sets are often cumbersome to work with. Ensure that students have

a goal of developing a scientific explanation, grounded in the data, for addressing the investigative question. For example, in a pond study this explanation could address whether or not the water is safe to use in different ways (swimming, fishing, for livestock, etc.) or could explain historical trends in the data (evidence that pollution is getting better or worse). This explanation would likely provide details of mechanisms that drive water quality (e.g., eutrophication), and use data to support its claims.

(4) Provide an opportunity to develop a culminating experience or a final artifact.
Have students create a final artifact or participate in a culminating activity tied to the explanation. This could be participation in a debate or creation of a poster or PowerPoint presentation. The intent of the culminating experience is to provide learners with the opportunity to communicate their findings to an audience. In the pond study example, a presentation could be given to a local government policy-making group.

(5) Provide flexibility.
Web-based inquiry projects should be flexible to promote active participation of classrooms. Be aware of the time demands of the project. Some projects are more flexible with deadlines for data gathering and submitting data than others.

Examples of Best Practice

Three examples follow that illustrate how WBIs may be used effectively in science classrooms.

Lehigh Earth Observatory (LEO) EnviroSci Inquiry

(*www.leo.lehigh.edu/envirosci*)
The LEO EnviroSci Inquiry is a comprehensive website at Lehigh University containing a variety of instructional materials designed to support investigations in the Lehigh River watershed. To motivate learners to understand an important aspect of watershed studies, a teacher has students complete the Dissolved Oxygen activity. This WBI activity highlights chemistry understanding and assists learners in understanding how to analyze and interpret water quality data. The teacher introduces the Lehigh River watershed by presenting MPEG movie watershed flybys located in the Lehigh River Watershed Photojournal to provide students with a graphical overview of the topography of the watershed area. GIS maps from the website are then shown to highlight how streams, tributaries, and the river connect to each other. Cities are added to the GIS map to illustrate population centers along the river.

In class, students use the Photojournal to virtually explore the area. They also look at the History of the Lehigh Watershed section to learn how science and technology have impacted the watershed over time. Prior to a water quality sampling trip to a nearby stream, students use the Water Quality website section to become familiar with water quality background information and probeware sampling protocols for data collection. Data is collected during a field trip to a stream and is then submitted to the LEO Partner Schools water quality database. The students' data is compared to other water quality data located in the database, including data from the same sampling location taken by the teacher's classes from previous years. The teacher prompts students to compare relationships between water quality variables. The students construct a series of posters highlighting their investigative findings of water quality in the watershed, and they present their posters to the public during the school's community outreach night.

Figure 1.

Home page for Lehigh River Watershed Explorations.
(*www.leo.lehigh.edu/envirosci/watershed*)

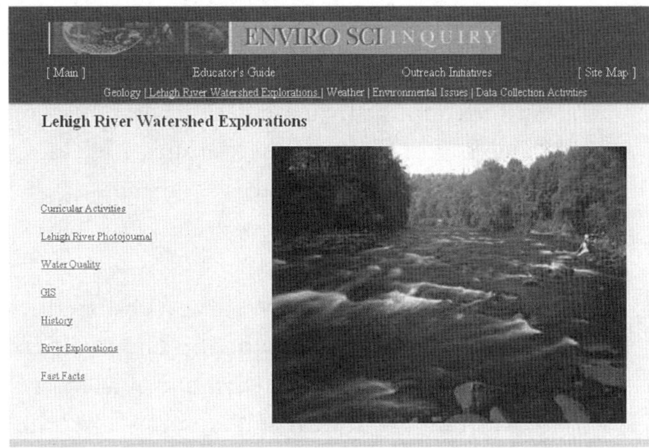

Human Genetics: Is the dominant trait most prevalent?
CEISE Collaborative Project website at the Stevens Institute of Technology's Center for Innovation in Engineering and Science Education
(*www.k12science.org/curriculum/genproj*)
The CEISE Collaborative Project is designed for students to investigate the prevalence of dominant alleles of particular human traits in the general population. Students are intrinsically motivated to investigate why some of their physical characteristics may differ from others. A teacher presents the students with the activity's driving question for the investigation. A classroom survey of select trait differences are conducted that include free or attached earlobes, curved or straight thumb, straight or bent pinky, and the presence or absence of white forelock, dimples, mid-digit hair, and colorblindness. The teacher then asks the students if they think the class data is characteristic of the general population. After a discussion about sample sizes, the teacher presents the Human Genetics web-based project and informs the students that their class data will be contributed to a much larger database containing traits from students across the

world. After the class data has been submitted and verified by the website's project staff, the students download the cumulative database as an Excel spreadsheet file. Students analyze the large data set and note the phenotype percentage displayed for each trait. Possible genotypes for each trait are discussed in class, and then students construct a data-supported response to the question, "Is the dominant trait most prevalent in the sampled population?" The class discusses what might cause a recessive trait to be more common in a population and posts a report describing the investigation to the "Final Reports" area of the website.

What's in a House?

(*http://wise.berkeley.edu*)

What's in a House? is a WISE (Web-based Inquiry Science Environment) curricular enhancement activity at the University of California, Berkeley, in which students design an energy-efficient house for a desert environment. In class, students are learning about heat and energy. To set the stage for the activity, the teacher asks the students to think of ways they might make their home more energy efficient. Next, the teacher introduces the WISE activity by asking the question, "What is the best way to design a desert home?" Students must design an energy-efficient house for a desert climate that will keep cool in the daytime and warm during the night. In groups, students complete a sequence of web-based activities to learn about plant adaptations for reflective surfaces, heat retention, and large heat capacity. Next, they apply these strategies as groups of students are assigned to design a roof, walls, or windows for a desert home based on evidence from their research on building materials. Each group presents their design to the rest of the class.

Conclusion

Web-based science inquiry projects take a variety of forms that include collaborative projects, curriculum enhancement activities, and comprehensive websites designed to support an in-depth study of a particular science topic or geographical area. Successful uses of WBI activities are enhanced if investigations are meaningful and relevant to students and take advantage of local phenomena to gain student interest. As the examples in this chapter illustrate, you may need to enhance a project with a more relevant, motivating context to assist with capturing the interest of your own students.

The primary learning environment for web-based activities is the classroom. Even though the WBIs described in this chapter are designed to promote inquiry learning, you are the most important person for structuring the inquiry process in the classroom. The inquiry process is enhanced when you provide appropriate prompts and suggestions for analyzing data, and promoting critical thinking and reasoning skills.

WEB-BASED INQUIRY ACTIVITY

One high school science class wanted to investigate the following research question: *How healthy is the creek next to our school?*

The teacher, Kate Prince, located a website from the state's Department of Natural Resources (DNR) that is designed to assist student watershed studies of local streams. The site contains many resources, including protocols for water quality data collection, links to Geographic Information Systems (GIS) maps containing environmental data, a database of water quality data collected by students from across the state, and information about watershed studies conducted by state scientists. The website also contains a link to a simulated creek investigation activity developed by a local university.

Kate decided this activity would present her students with a motivating context to conduct a local stream study while at the same time helping them to understand important water quality concepts better than the activities provided in the school-adopted textbook.

The students, with guidance from Kate, visited the creek one time during the fall, winter, and spring to obtain a seasonal data set. The class followed the website's procedures for using probeware to gather water quality data. The collected data was submitted to the DNR site using a provided web-based form. Kate used the prompts provided on the website to assist students with their data analysis:

- *What patterns do you observe?*
- *Does one variable seem to be related to another?*
- *Is this what you would expect to see? Why or why not?*
- *What about the outliers? Where do they come from? Why?*
- *Can you see changes over time?*

One group noticed related data from a nearby school participating in the DNR watershed project. In class discussion, the students decided to use the GIS maps and collected stream and tributary data from other schools located in the river's watershed to look for additional data patterns. They discussed findings in class after the analysis was competed. Then, Kate prompted the students with questions to think about alternative explanations that may account for their findings. She reminded students that they can access relevant and reliable scientific knowledge from research scientists on the DNR website.

After additional research, students discovered information about two river tributaries contributing abandoned mine drainage. This information led to further class discussion about ways to remediate abandoned mine drainage to the river.

The student groups then submitted a written report of their investigation to the DNR website. The reports were displayed on the website along with other watershed study reports from schools across the state.

In many WBI activities, students investigate problems that are also studied by scientists. These activities require learners to use evidence and practices of the same type actual scientists use. These investigations are purposeful and a variety of scientific processes are emphasized. Science learning, therefore, becomes an active process that transforms the classroom into a place more closely resembling the working environment of scientists.

CHAPTER 8

Online Assessments and Hearing Students Think About Science

Taryn L. S. Hess and Sherry A. Southerland

Ellen, a student new to Parkview Middle School, was late to her first period science class. As she approached the door of the science classroom, she found the following note: "You can find Ms. Hannah's class at the computer lab," with an arrow indicating the direction of the lab. Ellen groaned to herself, knowing that she really didn't enjoy the computer assignments in her former school. As she had explained to a teacher, "At first they're pretty cool, but after you get used to doing your work on the computer, what's the difference between that and a worksheet?"

As she approached the computer lab, she was surprised to hear a number of students arguing. Upon entering the lab, Ellen saw about 30 students in the classroom, in groups of two or three, sitting in front of a computer screen. Why, she wasn't sure, as there were more computers available, sitting unused. Some groups of students were quietly reading the screen and whispering ideas to one another. Other students raised their voices, and gestured to one another over the tops of monitors.

"What did you get for that one?" a boy called out.

The four students sitting near him broke out in laughter, one exclaiming, "You know it doesn't work that way, man.... *His* right answer isn't *your* right answer," followed by more laughing.

The first speaker smiled a bit then offered in an overly deliberate voice, enunciating each word as if it was memorized from some often heard script, "Okay, okay. 'Can you explain your reasoning on this question?'"—then in a quicker, lighter tone, "'Cause the system is telling us we did something wrong and we can't figure it out."

In response, a girl from the group he was speaking to rose from her seat, leaned over the desk, and began offering an explanation.

Ellen scanned the room looking for the adult in this group, and found Ms. Hannah working in the back with a trio of students. As Ellen approached, Ms. Hannah was asking the trio, "So which one would sink if you placed it in water?"

One of the students called out "The wood. It's heavier."

Ms. Hannah made a note and looked back at the student and asked, "So you think that it's the weight, the mass, that determines if something is going to float?" Before the student could respond, Ms. Hannah took notice of her newest student.

When you think of online assessments, you, like Ellen, may envision students sitting alone in front of a computer screen silently clicking on answers to computer-generated questions. In this chapter we encourage you to consider a different use of online assessments—one that encourages collaboration and problem solving.

This chapter examines online assessments, and we hope to help you explore how these assessments might be useful in your science classroom. Although there is a wealth of computer-based assessment tools (such as homework and exam generation programs that accompany many science textbooks), the focus of this chapter is on a specific form of online, interactive assessments: specifically, web-based practice assignments in which students submit their work for computerized grading over the internet. These systems allow you to choose problems from a large bank of questions to assign to your class. They provide students instant feedback on the correctness of their responses, they give students the opportunity to re-attempt and correct answers, and they develop a unique assignment for every student. These programs even grade assignments for you. Online assessments can enhance science instruction by tapping into students' interest in computers and providing instant feedback on their efforts. They also provide valuable internet interaction and computer skills.

Although much of what we've just talked about is exactly what you would expect when thinking about online assessments, we want to describe a different aspect of such assessments. Just as the student from the introductory vignette observed, online assessments can go beyond simply having the student complete problem-solving drills. Assessment systems can allow students an avenue to talk through their growing science understandings, as well as providing you a venue to listen in on students' science ideas. In this chapter you'll get to see how online assessments can be an important tool in reform-based science.

Where can you find online assessments for science? Some large textbook publishers provide an online assessment feature if their book is adopted. Other publishers offer assessment packages to be used throughout the school year for a fee (see i-know by McGraw Hill and Quiz Lab by Pearson Education). Diagnoser Tools is a freely available, web-based assessment program that provides formative research-based assessments for a large number of science concepts (*www.diagnoser.com/diagnoser*).

On the high end of such programs are CAPA (Computer-Assisted Personalized Approach) or OASIS (Online Assessment and Integrated Study), which include a vast array of question banks and student responses. These programs are powerful but do take a bit of investment in terms of coming to understand how to use them.

Because of this, they can best be accessed through a local college or university, many of which use these programs in their undergraduate science courses.

Other than the system itself, associated costs of online assessments revolve around the actual hardware the students work on. Although students at home can use these assessments, decreasing the hardware requirements for your school, some groups of student have an easier time accessing up-to-date systems than others. Aside from the problem of differing access for students, the strengths of such programs are the discussion they can generate. If student discussion is your goal, then having a group of computers with simultaneous internet access is a must. Some classrooms may have access to multiple computers, but in most cases you'll need to access your school's computer lab. Although becoming familiar with any of these systems represents an investment (either in time or funding), we are excited by the way we have seen teachers take advantage of these systems through encouraging students to vocalize comprehension so their teachers can listen in.

What the Research Says

There is a growing body of research investigating the use of online assessment technologies, mostly conducted in college science courses. For example, in an early implementation of computerized homework in a large college physics course, Hudson (1985) reported a dramatic reduction in the number of course dropouts. He argued that this reduction was due to the value of homework in physics courses and the role of feedback in shaping student learning and success in the class. Hudson argued that the immediate assessment and instant feedback of these computerized homework systems clearly aided these students' learning and success in physics, thus decreasing their potential to drop out.

Walberg, Paschal, and Weinstein (1985) conducted a large-scale synthesis of a number of studies and found that homework that was graded or commented on had a large effect in shaping student learning, whereas homework without feedback had only a small effect on student learning. Based on this, we suggest that the strength of online assessment comes from its use of *feedback*. Because online assessments allow for immediate feedback, they can help shape student learning.

A significant benefit from the use of online assessment programs in the traditional sense is the amount of time and energy you, the teacher, saves. That said, research also indicates that these systems initially *increase* a teacher's workload. It's only after you create the initial problem sets and become used to the system that your workload is reduced (Morrissey, Kashy, and Tsai 1995).

In one of the few studies on online assessments in secondary schools, Hassler and a number of colleagues (Hassler et al. 2004) focused on the use of CAPA in high school physics. In their research they compared the learning of students who used online assessments and students who had traditional homework assignments. They determined that students' overall satisfaction regarding the value of homework increased as a result of using online assessments for a unit of science.

Online assessment systems can provide more practice for students along with immediate feedback, shaping student learning as they work to correct mistakes. However, there are potential drawbacks to this use of these systems:

- Some programs offer limited feedback.
- There is always the danger of multiple submissions by students so that they can use a "trial and error" approach to problem solving instead of a close analysis of knowledge applications.
- When used inappropriately, such systems may contribute to further impersonalization of a course, as a human grader is replaced with a computer.

Online assessments, when carefully selected and employed, can enhance student science learning, but as teachers we must be careful in our selection and use of these tools.

Guidelines for Best Practice

We think of "best practices" as those you employ as you teach science with the reforms in mind (AAAS 1990; NRC 1996). Such practices include the focus on a small number of important concepts so that students can develop a meaningful, applicable knowledge of those concepts, instruction based on student's prior knowledge, the use of student sensemaking of activities (through writing, talking, and argument) in building an understanding of scientific concepts. We suggest that you select and use online assessments in ways that allow students to make sense of scientific phenomena. The science reform documents call for classroom talk that is rich, that includes many voices (and not just that of the teacher or text), and that builds on itself to arrive at new conclusions.

What would the use of an online assessment look like in a reform-based classroom? In the classrooms we've studied, online assessments were employed by the teacher as a review for the students, as a means for her to check their understanding of a unit—a check informed in part by their discussions around the questions as well as students' answers to the questions themselves. In order for the teacher to listen in, the sessions were held during class in the school's computer lab. Although the labs were large enough to allow for one student per terminal, students in these sessions often worked with partners, and these partners felt free to ask others in the room for help—as was suggested in the opening vignette. By listening into the students' conversations, the teacher quickly assessed areas in which they struggled and needed more support. In addition, the teacher had the opportunity to circulate,

speaking with individual students to further understand their knowledge—information that was essential in honing classroom instruction.

Here are some guidelines that should inform the selection of an appropriate online assessment package in a reform-based classroom:

(1) Make sure there is a wealth of content to draw upon in the package.
The package should address a number of the science concepts you plan to teach, as well as having a large question bank for each of these concepts. The investment (both in terms of computer support and individual attention) required for a new system to become familiar and easy to use is simply too demanding to warrant a system that cannot be used on a consistent basis throughout the school year.

(2) Make sure the problem sets are randomized.
As shown in the introductory vignette the randomized nature of problem sets allows for students to work in class groups because the "right answer" will be different for everyone. Randomized sets allow students to discuss and focus on conceptual issues and less on pursuit of a single "right answer" (simply because there is no single right answer).

(3) Make sure that the feedback provided by the system is meaningful to your students and serves to shape student thinking.
The Diagnoser project asks students multiple-choice questions about a phenomenon, then follows their answer with another question designed to elicit their reasoning. This allows the student and teacher to recognize the students' understandings in an explicit manner. The CAPA program will tell the student if the answer is correct or incorrect, and if incorrect it can display feedback, hints, explanations, and links to other course material.

(4) Make sure the system has flexibility so that it can be adapted for the students', classroom's, and teacher's needs.
The system should allow you to adjust the amount of attempts students can use to answer questions. A multitude of "skill-level" questions need to be available in order to adjust to the learners and types of instruction.

Once you've *selected* a program, here are some guidelines for your *use* of it:

(5) At the beginning, use the technology during class sessions at the school's computer lab, assigning two or three students to a computer.
Allow for student talk during these work sessions. In turn, you should take advan-

tage of the time to listen into student sense-making and conducting one-on-one discussions with students.

(6) Assign online assessments as class work rather than homework, given the digital divide seen in many of our more economically diverse or disadvantaged classrooms.

This allows online assessments to be time for group sensemaking and prevents this technology from furthering the achievement gap of students from low-income homes.

(7) Model how to approach the questions and their answers several times before students attempt this work on their own.

By this, you can emphasize that the goal in working on the problem sets isn't to get the right answer by any means, but to check the soundness of student thinking.

(8) Be willing to "stick with it" and ask for support when needed.

It takes a good deal of time for teachers to become familiar and comfortable with an online assessment program. Consider adopting such programs as a department and be willing to discuss their use during the first year of use so you can work out the "kinks" in the system. Don't judge the effectiveness of a program based on one or two months of use.

Examples of Best Practice

In this section, we will discuss one example of an online assessment system that we are well acquainted with, pointing out what about its structure allows it to be useful in the secondary science classroom, as well as describing how it can be employed to optimize student understanding of science content.

We conducted a study on the use of CAPA in a middle school science class (Sybol and Southerland 2005). In this classroom, online assessments were used as a method of reviewing and reteaching concepts to students during school hours. As in the opening vignette, online assessment sessions were conducted in the school's computer lab, which provided the ability for students to work individually. But during these sessions, we noticed that students often "attacked" the problem sets together. When they needed help, they discussed the problems and equations with the other students in the class, something that happened all the time during our observations. The teacher had been using online assessments for several years. Why? She explained that this particular program fit her goals, and we noticed that her particular use of it also fit with the way she had her students "talk" in science.

The typical "talk" in this classroom was interactive, including many students' voices, all of which were in search of a single correct answer. In addition, one of the

Figure 1

Screenshot from CAPA online assessment.

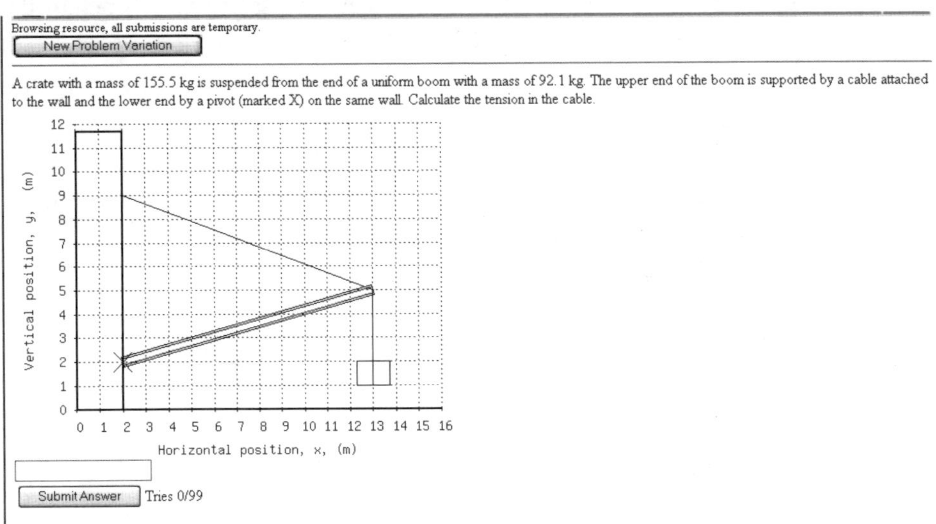

teacher's more general science teaching goals was to increase student collaboration. This goal was met through the online assessment, as during these sessions students were constantly collaborating with peers to answer problems. The online assessment also increased students' experiences with computers and the internet and increased their confidence in science activities.

Another of the benefits of this system is that it generates individualized student assignments. This feature allows for unique problems for a student, but with consistent concepts and principles being addressed for all the students in a class. This feature of generating individual assignments allows for students to work together in order to construct an understanding of the concepts but prevents them from simply sharing answers. This system provides instant feedback on students' responses, allowing them opportunities to reattempt and correct answers. The "no penalty" feature encourages students to understand, prompts students to correctly solve all the problems, and discourages students' random guessing. The intent here is to prevent students from relying on trial and error to achieve a correct response without developing an understanding of the underlying concepts. The characteristics interact in ways that allow students to quickly reshape their thinking.

The teacher in this classroom was accustomed to online assessments. Much of the initial investment of time and energy was already completed for her, so at the time of our observations her online assessment use had almost become second nature. This particular teacher valued understanding her students' thinking, and used their "talk" around the assessment problems to decide if the material had been adequately taught. Therefore, she ignored the myriad tasks sitting on her desk and used this time to focus on her students' sensemaking. In this regard, our teacher was different from many of her coworkers. Other teachers in her school began using the same online assessment program as an easy way to assign homework or to provide easy-to-record grades. Many of these teachers were far more used to having their voice primary in the classroom and were not used to listening to their students' thinking, and so they saw little value in listening to students think. Because of their preferred style of teaching, they found this online assessment didn't fit well in their classroom. It is not surprising that these same teachers stopped using the online assessment years ago.

Conclusion

What can we learn from this analysis of online assessments as tools of instruction? It is important to recognize that no one system fits all teachers. Online assessments must be selected based on how well they mesh with your own beliefs and common teaching practices. If there is not a suitable mesh, then you'll end up discarding the system. Based on this, systems need to be selected by teachers (not "handed down" to teachers). You need to select the program in terms of how well it fits your own teaching goals and the kinds of classroom talk you value.

Although online assessments can be an important part of a reform-based science classroom, it is important to recognize that these same tools can also be used in the pursuit of low-level knowledge, as a means of "drill and kill," and other forms of rote learning. If you are only using online assessments for individual homework assignments or as a means of testing students, then it is likely these tools will do little to deepen the understanding students have of science knowledge.

We close by urging you to look past the obvious in your consideration of online assessments. Yes, they have the potential to provide students with useful feedback and to decrease some aspects of your teaching work. But, more importantly, they can be a vital important tool in allowing you to listen in on your students thinking—thus providing invaluable information with which to craft your science instruction.

The Virtual Science Classroom

Tom Dana and Rick Ferdig

If virtual schooling has not already come to your school, it likely will soon. High schools throughout the world are increasingly providing courses in the physical, chemical, and biological sciences that are delivered in whole or in part by web-based distance learning technologies. These courses provide a unique opportunity for students to learn science at an accelerated pace or get a second chance at a course in which they may have failed or done poorly. Virtual schooling also offers students the opportunity to enroll in a science course not taught at their home school or school district, interact with expert instructors in a particular field, and gain access to subject matter they may have otherwise missed because of personal or instructional situations (i.e., teenage moms, home-schooled students, expelled students, etc.). The current interest in virtual schooling is intense, particularly because it is seen by some as a vehicle for increasing graduation rates and reducing dropout rates (Web-Based Education Commission 2000).

Those who question the reality of the virtual schooling movement need only to look at the current enrollments across the United States. Virtual High School (*www.govhs.org*), which began in 1996, now has over 200 online courses and 300 member schools, represented by 27 states and 24 international schools. Florida Virtual School (*www.flvs.net*), which started in 1997, served over 20,000 students in 2004–05. Furthermore, in 2005, the U.S. Department of Education estimated that 36% of school districts have students enrolled in distance education courses.

Many states have taken the lead by supporting statewide virtual school initiatives, while other states are leaving it up to individual schools or school districts to decide if and how to develop virtual schooling. As a consequence, high school teachers across the United States and around the world are now (or will soon be) exploring how to provide access to science for all students regardless of personal or institutional contexts or students' specific needs (i.e., remedial or advanced placement).

Virtual science classes typically offer opportunities for learning to take place through individual review of online lectures, virtual and at-home laboratory activities, and student-to-student as well as student-to-teacher interaction. Virtual schools are considered flexible because students can access course content 24 hours a day, 7 days a week, and nearly all year round. Students can proceed at a pace comfortable for their learning needs and can choose to engage with online lectures or do laboratories or assignments as they wish. Virtual science courses often integrate electronic resources into the course design that have been found to be effective with science learners. For example, websites that provide visualizations of scientific phenomenon such as remote sensing and image processing information for Earth science students are easy to embed into the online course environment. In a similar manner, any website can be brought into a course as a resource for learners. Figure 1 is a screen capture from an online science course that links out to the PBS Online website for a desired resource about air pressure.

Figure 1.

Importing web resources into a virtual science course.

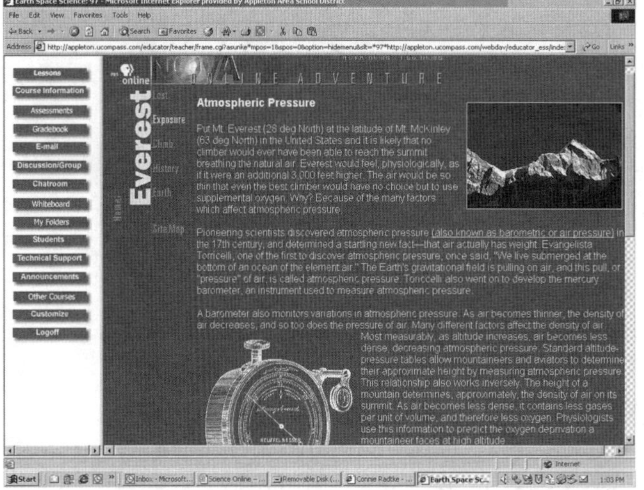

What the Research Says

Minimal research has been completed in the area of K–12 online schooling (Cavanaugh et al. 2004). There is evidence to suggest that students score equally well on exams in both virtual classrooms and face-to-face classrooms (Blomeyer 2002). Studies have also found that online courses enhance learner independence and foster higher-order thinking (Tal and Hochberg 2003). Furthermore, parents report positive perceptions of online courses because they have the ability to access assignments and grades and to be more aware of what tasks the student is completing, allowing the parent to offer assistance and facilitate learning expectations (Chaney 2001).

Being a relatively new phenomenon, virtual science classrooms have not been extensively studied. Questions unique to science education need investigation to determine if virtual science classes are useful for all students. In addition, future research needs to examine how and when various technologies can be useful in the virtual science classroom.

One important finding that has come from the research is the importance of what is known as *component architecture*. Component architecture essentially refers to implementing online lessons as a collection of smaller modules using a variety of technologies to deliver the content (Ferdig, Mishra, and Zhao 2004). This type of design allows for a more constructivist learning environment, with students having the opportunity to work on their interest areas or to receive remedial support in their specific area of need. The concept gained popularity in the last decade as educators began to discuss the possibility of reusable learning objects. If two different teachers were teaching chemistry online, for example, it would be foolish for each of them to build their own Periodic Table of the Elements. Multimedia Educational Resource for Learning and Online Teaching (Merlot; *www.merlot.org*) is one example of a repository of reusable learning objects where teachers can share such online content; science simulations, animations, tutorials, and other classroom materials for free.

In this chapter, we examine best teaching practices emerging within this new field and then showcase specific examples of how various technologies are used within virtual science classrooms.

Guidelines for Best Practices

Teaching science online requires a new set of teaching skills, although underlying principles of classroom-based science teaching such as a constructivist philosophy equally apply to facilitating science learning online. For example, both classroom-based and virtual science teachers need to scaffold students' scientific inquiry, set and communicate high expectations, and facilitate tasks that encourage active learning. Yet, new instructional strategies and approaches to teaching also are needed.

(1) Encourage active learning.

Although some virtual schools create their own science courses, a common pattern among emerging virtual schools is to purchase or license courses that have already been developed by existing schools. For example, the Appleton (Wisconsin) eSchool (*http://appleton.ucompass.com*), which began serving students in 2002–2003, provides online science course options that were licensed from Florida Virtual School, as well as courses that were developed locally. Often, courses are designed with activities, projects, lecture, assignments, and examinations in the absence of the actual instructor.

In a good course design, learning expectations are made clear to students, activities and assignments are clearly relevant to all possible students, exemplary course or online resources are built into the course, and appropriate assessment tools are used. Course design also should include clearly stated expectations about how long assignments may take to complete, assignment sequencing, and a calendar or automated reminders about due dates.

Online instructors of many prefabricated courses do not have the advantage of making last-minute changes in lectures, course resources, or assignments. In many courses, decisions about activity structures are made well before a course goes online. As a consequence, many teachers of virtual science classrooms have little control over major course components. But teachers do have flexibility and their pedagogical expertise can shine in the ways in which they foster communication to scaffold student learning.

(2) Encourage teacher-to-student interaction.

Online instructors may be best described as mediators of learning. They understand learning goals for students and provide opportunities for students to reach those goals. In virtual science classrooms, the teacher can structure learning tasks, open discussions with provocative questions, invite student participation, facilitate group collaboration, provide electronic mentoring, point to additional online resources, and structure transitions between learning activities. Many times the teacher's work is done through posts to discussion forums or via e-mail, although most virtual schools also expect teachers to be in regular phone contact with students. Although some online learning environments offer synchronous communications opportunities such as live "chat" or instant messaging, a defining feature in most online learning environments is asynchronicity. With asynchronous communications, students engage with the learning materials at their own pace and interact with peers and instructors via e-mail and discussion boards at a time convenient for their schedules.

Although 24/7 access to instructors via electronic communications is unparalleled, many teachers find that students expect immediate responses to their queries. With experience, online teachers learn to specify or limit the times they communicate via e-mail or web postings. Effective instructor e-mail response policies may include specific guidelines, such as "All posts will be answered within 24 hours on weekdays only." Since most communication is handled through text, effective online teachers develop a consistent style, tone, and format for messages to students.

(3) Encourage student-to-student interaction.

In addition to communications from the teacher, virtual courses often require student cooperation and communication. Student interaction can vary from simple e-mail exchanges between two students in a study group to a series of messages between students engaged in drawing conclusions from an analysis of, for example, an online database of buoy data (e.g., the National Data Buoy Center website at *www.ndbc.noaa.gov*). A significant task for teachers whose online courses require student-to-student interaction is maintenance of group activities, often requiring explicit directions to students about how to interact and cooperate asynchronously in order to achieve the specified learning goals.

Teachers should post examples of excellent student discussions and provide feedback to students to help them improve their online discussion abilities. Selecting interaction structures and having a set of teaching strategies that fosters student-to-student interaction is important. Most online learning environments have multiple communication structures available (i.e., public, private, topical grouping, forums, town halls, etc.) The discussion structure chosen should be simple and easy for students to navigate. Teaching strategies such as providing a specific task to focus an online discussion or arranging the discussion like a debate can also help. Since students typically do not have a minimal period of time they are expected to be online, the structure and teaching strategies can keep students engaged until an assignment is completed.

(4) Encourage students to create and collect artifacts.
Creating artifacts (representations of student knowledge and understanding) allows students to learn concepts, apply information, and represent knowledge in a variety of ways. Artifacts represent students' understanding of the problem, their solutions, and the knowledge they gained. For example, in Project-Based Science (*www.umich.edu/~pbsgroup*), students use scientific tools to manipulate and revise video, audio, text, and graphics in the creation of their artifacts. These artifacts can then be collected in an electronic portfolio, a repository of artifacts representing student knowledge growth over time.

Examples of Best Practice

Active learning, interaction, and artifact creation are all best practice strategies that can be implemented online using various technologies. Perhaps the best way to showcase online science classrooms using those strategies is to present examples of the various components used in such a class. The components in virtual science classrooms include lectures, videos, discussions, inquiry assignments, simulations, and laboratories.

Lectures tend to be text based with a sprinkling of graphics. Often, links are embedded in the lectures to static and dynamic images or external websites with relevant content. These lectures often take the form of recorded PowerPoint presentations, and they can be accompanied by response assignments. One example of the online lecture is the Connecting Concepts project at the University of Wisconsin (*http://ats.doit.wisc.edu/biology/lessons.htm*). These online lessons in biology provide students with text and graphics followed by a table to check their understanding. Lectures can also be delivered via video presentation, which can take the form of entire lectures or video examples of science experiments. The Vega Science Trust (*www.vega.org.uk*) has interviews with Nobel Prize winners as well as lectures from eminent scientists. Discovery School's section on Physical Sciences (*http://school.discoveryeducation.com/ontv/videoclips/physicalsci1.html*) has smaller video clips aimed at such things as the elements, force and motion, and the human brain. Steve Spangler Science (*www.stevespanglerscience.com/video*) has free videos that offer ideas for science lessons. Teachers could utilize shorter or longer clips from these free online resources to supplement their online instruction.

Discussions follow various formats. They can be asynchronous, with students and teachers posting when they have time. Or they can be synchronous, with participants each logging in at the same time. Asynchronous discussions provide an opportunity for questions and answers to be posted for all participants to see. Synchronous chats provide just-in-time support. Both provide opportunities for science teachers to assign group work and to monitor the group interactions. These discussions often take place within the online course. However, teachers may decide to have students connect to participants outside of the classroom. The Science Chat Forum (*www.sciencechatforum.com*) is an example of a multidisciplinary website for chatting about science topics.

The inquiry assignment is a third component within online classrooms. These assignments provide students with an opportunity to take ownership of asking important questions, investigating solutions, and reflecting on results. Chip Bruce at the University of Illinois has created the "Inquiry Page" (*http://inquiry.uiuc.edu*). These web pages highlight inquiry, but also provide students with a place to post inquiry projects. A science search yields inquiry projects ranging from Biology Workbenches to Biodiversity. A second example of online inquiry, and one that is familiar to most teachers, is the webquest. A webquest is an inquiry activity in which students use the web to provide solutions to suggested problems or questions. Many teachers like webquests because they provide directed web-based activities for students. Webquests can be found at (*http://webquest.org*); teachers can use submitted webquests or they can contribute their own.

Simulations as a fourth component of online science classes are probably the most widely known because teachers use them in both face-to-face and online classes (see Chapter 3). Simulations are different from virtual labs in that labs use simulations and other components to form lessons; simulations are often smaller and more specific explorations.

Laboratories in virtual science classrooms tend to be one of two types: the virtual lab and the at-home lab. One example of a virtual lab in an online science course is shown in Figure 2. In this lab, students are asked to observe a picture of a slide with cells from an onion root. Students are asked to observe and note certain features, record their observations, and then draw conclusions by answering a series of provided questions. A report is then e-mailed to the teacher for feedback and grading.

Another common laboratory is the type students complete at home with materials found around the typical home. An example is shown in Figure 3. In the Effects of Air Pressure lab, students are provided with instructions to perform an investigation using a soda can, stovetop, and other household items. Students conduct the activity independently, answer the questions, and submit a report.

Other possible formats for laboratory investigations are possible, but not generally seen in virtual science classrooms to date. Teachers who have the flexibility to alter course assignments and designers of new virtual science classes may want to consider strategies such as having students share data collected individually and prepare a group report that clearly uses data to support conclusions or having them access existing data from a website.

Figure 2.

Example of a virtual lab in an online science course.

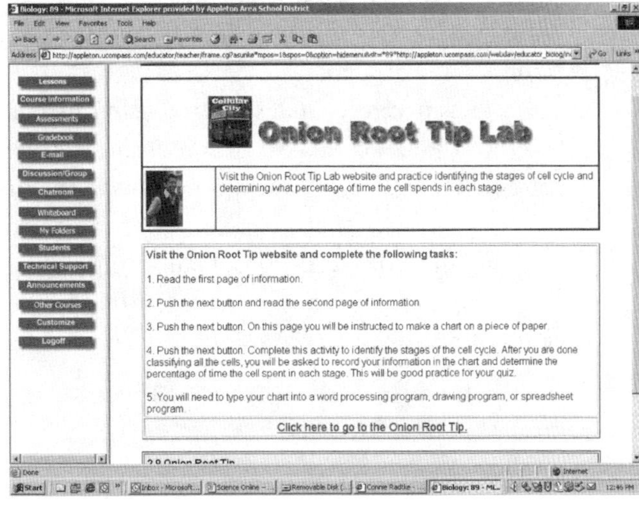

Figure 3.

Example of an "at home" laboratory.

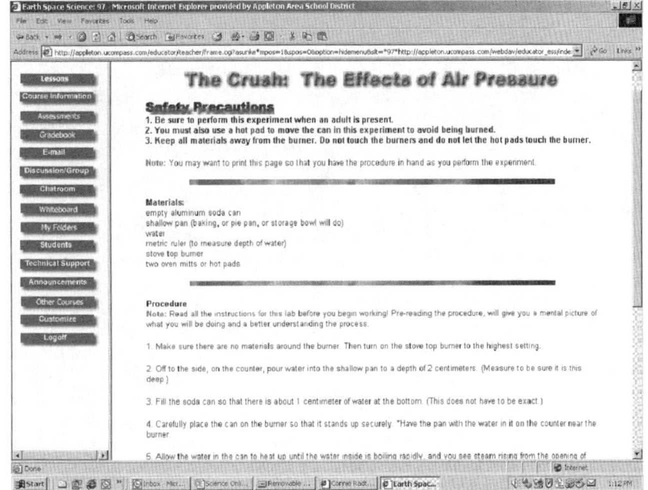

Conclusion

Although one of the greatest benefits to virtual science courses is the access it provides to students, some caution is warranted. Students who are science-phobic, have limited English language abilities, or require accommodations for specific disabilities will need special attention if they are to be successful in virtual science classrooms. In the NSTA position statement, "Gender Equity in Science Education," science teachers are admonished to "select only those curriculum materials that present culturally diverse male and female role models working in all disciplines and at all levels of science." To make science content accessible for all students enrolled in a virtual science course, the teacher may need to add or change curriculum materials, online course resources, or links to external websites that are not accessible to students with specific disabilities. Such an act is not easy in most virtual school environments.

The current virtual science teacher usually has more control of communications methods than actual course content. It is critical, therefore, that teachers master the discussion and communications tools in the online learning environment and know how to use those tools to create accommodations that will reach all learners. By posing higher-order questions, facilitating dialogue, and finding or creating accessible learning materials that meet individual learner needs, instructors can be successful in helping all students of virtual science classes become most successful.

CHAPTER 10

Technology's Greatest Value

Randy L. Bell and Glen Bull

The educational materials developer William Pflaum (2004) wanted to witness the ways technology in schools had transformed education. He visited a cross-section of schools across the nation, observing classrooms and talking with teachers, students, technology specialists, and administrators. His book, *The Technology Fix: The Promise and Reality of Computers in Our Schools,* records his findings.

Pflaum was mostly disappointed by what he saw. Among his conclusions, he noted that teachers know how to use productivity tools but the skill "does not necessarily carry over to the effective use of computers for instruction." He also noted that "too much time is spent on the mechanics of computer-based tools and too little time is spent on the content being studied" (pp. 196–197). He placed the types of computer use he observed into five categories:

- **Computer as Teaching Machine.** Pflaum observed in a few classrooms students using "skill-building games, intervention activities, simulations, and test-prep materials" (p. 190), mostly in lower grades and often, in his opinion, ineffectively. With rare exception, the computer when used this way was intended to temporarily relieve the teacher of some teaching task.
- **Computer Productivity Tool.** Most often, especially in middle schools and high schools. Pflaum found students using computers as a "report writer, presentation giver, digital graphics tool, and communications hub." In some cases, teachers were convinced that the PowerPoint presentations students created taught them much about the target content, but most often student thought and energy seemed to be going into "exploring the mechanics of the software instead of the content" (p. 192).
- **Computer as Internet Portal.** Pflaum saw some teachers using the internet to give students access to information—sometimes information "they could not

have found within any school's four walls" (p. 193). In some cases students used the web to capture images and sound files to place in their PowerPoint presentations. The most "exceptional" activity he observed was students creating their own web pages based on the material drawn from a list of prequalified websites.

- **Computer as Test Giver.** Infrequently, Pflaum observed schools using computer-based testing. He saw this use as most attractive for high-stakes assessment because it allows for quicker reporting of results.
- **Computer as Data Processor.** A few administrators Pflaum spoke with viewed the primary role of computers as providing the data that drove their curriculum and administrative decisions.

In essence, Pflaum's investigation revealed schools as places where computers are ubiquitous, but are used primarily for administrative tasks and low-level instruction that emphasizes traditional instructional approaches. Although his work consists of unsystematic observations and anecdotes, Pflaum's findings largely parallel the research findings of Larry Cuban's (2001) earlier investigation. Technology in schools has, at best, tended to support traditional instruction, rather than rising to its potential to transform the ways teachers teach and students learn. At worst, technology in schools has been relegated primarily to administrative tasks, with little or no impact on classroom instruction.

A series of studies by the Pew Foundation on the Internet and American Life has systematically documented the way in which technology is affecting society and schools. In contrast to the somewhat pedestrian uses of technology in schools, these studies report that students are using technology extensively and in innovative ways outside of school. The authors conclude that there is a "digital disconnect" between limited use of technology in schools and extensive use of technology by students to complete academic work outside of school.

Using Technology Effectively in the Science Classroom

In contrast to technology uses Pflaum observed, this monograph describes a vision in which technology is used to facilitate data collection and analysis, to enhance scientific understandings through imagery and visualization, and to extend inquiry through communication and collaboration. Many of these uses of technology in science instruction are supported by a solid base of research evidence showing their value for improving student understanding.

The technology uses described here are powerful and effective because they follow a common philosophy, explicit in many of the individual chapter guidelines for best practice and implicit in the example activities. In general, these guidelines and examples emphasize

(1) keeping the focus on the science content rather than the mechanics of the technology;
(2) using technology in ways that are consistent with appropriate pedagogy, including opportunities for inquiry learning;
(3) using technology in ways that allow teachers and students to do what would otherwise be difficult to do without technology; and
(4) taking advantage of technology's power to engage student participation and interest.

Essentially, technology use in the science classroom is most effective when it encourages deeper student engagement with science content, when it is used to support rather than replace what we know about effective science instruction, and especially when it stretches the boundaries of what is possible in the science classroom.

Inquiry and Technology

A national consensus has established the central role of inquiry in science education. In fact, the National Science Education Standards (NSES) place inquiry "at the heart of science and science learning" (NRC 1996, p.15). As described in the NSES, inquiry into student-generated questions is a fundamental strategy for teaching science.

When thinking of inquiry, most teachers focus on real phenomena, whether in classroom instruction, in laboratory settings, or outdoors. The individual chapters of this book present a range of ideas and strategies supporting inquiry into real phenomena in each of these settings. However, as students engage in more abstract and complex topics, they soon reach the point at which exploring real phenomena is impractical or even impossible. This is the point at which the capabilities of computer-based technologies stand out. Teachers can engage students in inquiry as they guide students in acquiring and interpreting information from secondary sources, including internet databases and computer simulations.

Still, the way in which these resources are used is critical—using the internet as a convenient source of authoritative information is no better than using the textbook as the final authority. Neither approach emphasizes scientific inquiry as a powerful way to build knowledge.

In addition to *doing* inquiry, the NSES also emphasize developing understandings *about* inquiry as an essential component of scientific literacy. Thus, students should not only learn how to perform and design scientific investigations, but they should learn scientific habits of mind and the variety of ways scientists approach their investigations. Unfortunately, textbook approaches to science instruction often lead students to see scientific inquiry as an algorithm—the mythic "scientific method." Students dutifully learn the "five steps" of the scientific method as if it were a creed. Yet, scientific inquiry is so much richer than any algorithm!

Appropriate uses of technology have the potential to let students experience and learn about a wide variety of approaches to scientific problem solving. As the resources provided in this book demonstrate, technology in the hands of creative teachers can expand the range of ways students see science and experience first-hand the joy of discovery and the creative thinking that goes into planning investigations. By experiencing the creative, problem-solving side of scientific work, they are more likely to see scientific investigations as relevant or meaningful. Thus, in the hands of a skillful teacher, computer-based technologies can provide students with an interactive, educational environment for both thinking about and doing scientific investigations.

The Unnatural Nature of Science

One major challenge of science instruction is that many scientific ideas are complex, abstract, and contrary to everyday experience, making them difficult for students to understand. As Wolpert (1992) explained,

> I would almost contend that if something fits in with common sense it almost certainly isn't science. The reason again, is that the way in which the universe works is not the way in which common sense works: the two are not congruent. (p. 11)

The large body of literature on misconceptions supports the idea that learning science is neither straightforward nor consistent with students' everyday experiences (e.g., Driver et al. 1994). These nonintuitive ideas present science teachers with pedagogical challenges. Developing the skills for making scientific views more accessible is an example of "pedagogical content knowledge" (Shulman 1987). Teachers, Shulman argued, may be distinguished from other professionals by their ability to link knowledge of content, instruction, learners, and curriculum.

As the chapters in this book have shown, technology provides unique opportunities to address these challenges, but only when used in conjunction with effective teaching practices. Technology use can be seen as a means to an end (student learning), but never the end in itself. The bottom line is that it's not about the technology. It's about how teachers use the technology. Even with all of the promising new technologies available today, the teacher is still (and always will be) the most important part of the equation.

Scientific Information and the Web

Much of the knowledge people use every day is closely linked to science and the ways scientific knowledge is produced. They use this knowledge to solve problems creatively, think critically, work cooperatively in teams, and use technology effectively. In fact, one indicator of scientific literacy is the ability to use scientific principles and processes in making personal decisions (NRC 1996).

Evolving information technologies are presenting opportunities for more people to incorporate science in their everyday lives. The Pew Foundation (Horrigan 2006) reports that fully 87% of online users (128 million adults) have made use of the internet to conduct research on a scientific topic or concept. The positive aspect of this finding is that users are interested in science and in making use of the internet to pursue this interest—over half have used the web to check a scientific fact or statistic, and nearly as many have downloaded scientific data, graphs, or charts from the internet.

However, the conclusions of this study also suggest that happenstance is currently a significant factor in the sources of this information and the way in which it is acquired on the internet. Science educators could clearly make important contributions in preparing young citizens to use this evolving resource effectively.

Looking Ahead

The technologies discussed in this monograph were chosen to cover a cross-section of contemporary tools that were accompanied by research evidence indicating they help students engage in relevant learning of important science concepts. In the brief span of time from conception to publication of the monograph, new web capabilities have swept a generation of computer users into an era that has been characterized as an *Age of Participation*.

As the Pew Foundation has documented, 21st-century users are creating and disseminating content through a variety of internet channels that did not previously exist. These media include text (e.g., web logs, or blogs), sound (e.g., podcasts), images (e.g., Flickr), and video (e.g., YouTube). These activities are facilitated by the integration of data gathering sensors in a variety of mobile devices—digital cameras, cell phones, handhelds, GPS devices, and MP3 players. Many of these devices embody multiple functions. For example, many MP3 players can record as well as play sound, and it is increasingly common for cell phones to include digital cameras, GPS sensors, and video recorders. These handheld devices are portable digital data acquisition and communication devices, the least powerful of which has more computing power and memory than the mission control mainframe that guided the first trip to the Moon!

These activities are fueled by an emerging generation of Web 2.0 tools and technologies now available at no cost or low cost to consumers. These capabilities increase the usability and decrease the cost of technologies discussed in this monograph. For example, MotionBox, JumpCut, and VideoEgg offer free websites that let people upload, store, and edit videos with such features as transitions and captioning. As the web itself becomes a platform, schools will not always need to purchase expensive site licenses and install software applications on every computer. Students (and teachers) can have access to their digital video projects anytime, anywhere they can get to a computer and an internet connection.

It remains to be seen if and how these capabilities can be harnessed to engage students effectively in relevant science learning. Creative science teachers may discover ways to use for science purposes the data acquisition capabilities in many cell phones. Or they may even figure out how to take educational advantage of students' interest in photographing and filming themselves—as evidenced through the popularity of sites like MySpace and Facebook—and posting their thoughts and opinions on blogs.

Technology is changing at such a rapid pace that you can be sure that even more new capabilities will arise before you have figured out all the ways to use the tools presented in this book. Indeed, the main value of this book may be in helping you form a philosophy for determining when bringing technology into the science classroom is worthwhile and a set of principles to guide you when you deem it so.

Digital technologies are so pervasive in the practice of science that to ignore them altogether would be unfair to students growing up in the 21st century. Scientists certainly use technology for writing reports, giving presentations, and communicating with others. Yet, technology's greatest value has been in helping scientists make incredible leaps in understanding the world around them. Technology at times may also serve the same purpose for your students. There will always be a cost in dollars and in time when you bring technology into the classroom, but we hope we have given you some tools for determining when the cost is worth the learning that will result.

References

Akpan, J. P., and T. Andre. 2000. Using a computer simulation before dissection to help students learn anatomy. *Journal of Computers in Mathematics and Science Teaching* 19 (3): 297–313.

American Association for the Advancement of Science (AAAS). 1990. *Science for all Americans: Project 2061.* New York: Oxford University Press.

Baker, T. R. 2002. *The effects of geographic information system (GIS) technologies on students' attitudes, self-efficacy, and achievement in middle school science classrooms.* Unpublished doctoral dissertation. The University of Kansas, Lawrence.

Bayraktar, S. 2002. A meta-analysis of the effectiveness of computer-assisted instruction in science education. *Journal of Research on Technology in Education 34 (2): 173–188.*

Blomeyer, R. 2002. *Online learning for K–12 students: What do we know now?* Available online from the Learning Point Associates website at *www.ncrel.org/tech/elearn/synthesis.pdf.*

Bodzin, A., and W. Cates. 2002. Inquiry dot com: Web-based activities promote scientific inquiry learning. *The Science Teacher* 69 (9): 48–52.

Bodzin, A., and L. Shive. 2004. Designing for watershed inquiry. *Applied Environmental Education and Communication* 3 (4): 249–258.

Boster, F. J., G. S. Meyer, A. J. Roberto, C. Inge, and R. Strom. 2006. Some effects of video streaming on educational achievement. *Communication Education* 55: 46–62.

Bransford, J. D. 1979. *Human cognition*. Belmont, CA: Wadsworth Publishing.

Bransford, J. D., and M. K. Johnson. 1972. Contextual prerequisites for understanding: Some investigations of comprehension and recall. *Journal of Verbal Learning and Verbal Behavior* 11: 717–726.

Brassell, H. 1987. The effect of real-time laboratory graphing on learning graphic representations of distance and velocity. *Journal of Research in Science Teaching* 24 (4): 385–395.

Bush, V. 1945. As we may think. *The Atlantic Monthly* 176 (1): 101–108. Also available at *www.theatlantic.com/doc/194507/bush*

Cavanaugh, C., K. J. Gillan, J. Kromrey, M. Hess, and R. Blomeyer. 2004. *The effects of distance education on K–12 student outcomes: A meta-analysis.* Available online from the Learning Point Associates website at *www.ncrel.org/tech/distance/index.html.*

Chaney, E. G. 2001. Web-based instruction in a rural high school: A collaborative inquiry into its effectiveness and desirability. *NASSP Bulletin* 85: 20–35.

Crabb, K. 2001. *Case study of geographic information system integration in a high school world geography classroom*. Unpublished doctoral dissertation. The University of Georgia, Athens.

Cuban, L. 2001. *Oversold and underused: Computers in the classroom*. Cambridge, MA: Harvard University Press.

Dale, E. 1969. *Audiovisual methods in teaching*. New York: Holt, Rinehart and Winston.

Doering, A. 2002. GIS in education: An examination of pedagogy. *The ESRI User Conference 2002 proceedings*. Redlands, CA: ESRI Press.

Driver, R., A. Squires, P. Rushworth, and V. Wood-Robinson. 1994. *Making sense of secondary science: Research into children's ideas.* New York: Routledge.

Feldman, A., C. Konold, and R. Coulter, with B. Conroy, C. Hutchison, and N. London. 2000. *Network science, a decade later: The internet and classroom learning*. Mahwah, NJ: Lawrence Erlbaum Associates.

Ferdig, R. E., P. Mishra, and Y. Zhao. 2004. Component architectures and web-based learning environments. *Journal of Interactive Learning Research* 15 (1): 75–90.

Findahl, O. 1971. *The effect of visual illustrations upon perception and retention of new programmes.* Stockholm: Swedish Broadcasting Corporation. (ERIC Document Reproduction Service No. ED 054 631)

Flick, L., and R. Bell. 2000. Preparing tomorrow's science teachers to use technology: Guidelines for Science educators. *Contemporary Issues in Technology and Teacher Education* 1 (1). Available online at *www.citejournal.org/vol1/iss1/currentissues/science/article1.htm*

Geban, O., P. Askar, and I. Ozkan. 1992. Effects of computer simulations and problem-solving approaches on high school students. *Journal of Educational Research* 86 (1): 5–10.

Gorsky, P., and M. Finegold. 1992. Using computer simulations to restructure students' conceptions of force. *Journal of Computers in Mathematics and Science Teaching* 11: 163–178.

Harrison, A., and O. deJong. 2005. Exploring the use of multiple analogical models when teaching and learning chemical equilibrium. *Journal of Research in Science Teaching* 42 (10): 1135–1159.

Hassler, L., L. Dennis, H. Ng, C. Johnson, D. Ossont, G. Ogawa, and C. Nahmias. 2004. Computer-assisted vs. traditional homework: Results of a pilot research project. In *Human perspectives in the internet society: Culture, psychology, and gender*, eds. K. Morgan, C. A. Brebbia, J. Sanchez, and A. Voiskounsky, 467–478. Southampton, UK: WIT Press.

Hoban, C. F., and E. B. van Ormer. 1951. Instructional film research: 1918–1950. (Technical Report No. SDC-269-7-19, NAVEXOS P-977). Port Washington, NY: Special Devices Center.

Horrigan, J. 2006. *The internet as a resource for news and information about science. Washington, DC: Pew Internet and the American Life Project*. Available online at *www.pewinternet.org/pdfs/PIP_Exploratorium_Science.pdf*

Hsu, Y., and R. Thomas. 2002. The impacts of a web-aided instructional simulation on science learning. *International Journal of Science Education* 24 (9): 955–979.

Hudson, H. T. 1985. Teaching physics to a large lecture section. *Physics Teacher* 23: 88.

Hunter, B., and Y. Xie. 2001. Data tools for real-world learning. *Learning and Leading With Technology* 28 (7): 18–24.

Kerski, J. J. 2000. *The implementation and effectiveness of geographic information systems technology and methods in secondary education*. Unpublished doctoral dissertation. University of Colorado, Boulder.

Kulik, J. 2002. *School mathematics and science programs benefit from instructional technology* (InfoBrief). Washington, DC: National Science Foundation. Available online at *www.nsf.gov/sbe/srs/infbrief/nsf03301/start.htm*

Lee, H., and B. Songer. 2003. Making authentic science accessible to students. *International Journal of Science Education* 25 (8): 923–948.

Lenk, C. 1992. The network science experience: Learning from three major projects. In *Prospects for educational telecomputing: Selected readings,* eds. R. Tinker, and P. Kapisovsky, 51–60. Cambridge, MA: Technical Education Research Center.

Levie, W. H., and R. Lentz. 1982. Effects of text illustrations: A review of research. *Educational Communication and Technology* 30 (4): 195–232.

Levin, J. R. 1989. A transfer-appropriate-processing perspective of pictures in prose. In *Knowledge acquisition from text and pictures,* eds. H. Mandl, and J. R. Levin, 83–100. Amsterdam: Elsevier Science.

Levin, J. R., G. J. Anglin, and R. N. Carney. 1987. On pictures in prose. *Education, Communication, and Technology* 27: 233–243.

Lynch, M. P., and A. Walton. 1998. Talking trash on the internet: Working real data into your classroom. *Learning and Leading With Technology* 25 (5): 26–31.

McNeil, B. J., and K. R. Nelson. 1991. Meta-analysis of interactive video instruction: A 10 year review of achievement effects. *Journal of Computer-Based Instruction* 18: 1–6.

Means, B., and K. Olson. 1995. *Technology's role within constructivist classrooms*. Paper presented at the annual meeting of the American Educational Research Association, San Francisco.

Mintz, R. 1993. Computerized simulations as an inquiry tool. *School Science and Mathematics 93* (2): 76–80.

Mistler-Jackson, M., and B. Songer. 2000. Student motivation and internet technology: Are students empowered to learn science? *Journal of Research in Science Teaching* 37 (5): 459–479.

Morrissey, D. J., E. Kashy, and I. Tsai. 1995. Using computer-assisted personalized assignments for freshman chemistry. *Journal of Chemical Education* 72 (2): 141–146.

National Research Council (NRC). 1996. *National science education standards*. Washington, DC: National Academy Press.

National Research Council (NRC). 2000. *Inquiry and the national science education standards: A guide for teaching and learning*. Washington, DC: National Academy Press.

National Research Council (NRC). 2006. *Learning to think spatially*. Washington, DC: National Academy Press.

Olsen, T. 2000. *Situated student learning and spatial informational analysis for environmental problem*. Unpublished doctoral dissertation. The University of Wisconsin.

Pflaum, W. D. 2004. *The technology fix: The promise and reality of computers in our schools.* Alexandria, VA: Association for Supervision and Curriculum Development.

Royuk, B., and D. W. Brooks. 2003 Cookbook procedures in MBL physics exercises. *Journal of Science Education and Technology* 12 (3): 317–324.

Russell, D. W., K. B. Lucas, and C. J. McRobbie. 2003. The role of the microcomputer-based laboratory display in supporting the construction of new understandings in kinematics. *Research in Science Education* 33 (2): 217–243.

Shulman, L. S. 1987. Knowledge and teaching: Foundations of the new reform. *Harvard Educational Review* 57: 1–22.

Slater, T. F., and B. Beaudrie. 1998. Doing real science on the web: Bringing authentic investigations to your classroom. *Learning and Leading with Technology* 25 (4): 28–31.

Slater, T. F., and L. Fixen. 1998. Two models for K–12 hypermediated Earth system science lessons based on internet resources. *School Science and Mathematics* 98: 35–40.

Slykhuis, D. A. 2004. *The efficacy of world wide web-mediated microcomputer-based laboratory activities in the high school physics classroom.* Doctoral Dissertation, North Carolina State University.

Snow, J. 1856. Cholera and the water supply of the south districts of London in 1854. *Journal of Public Health* 2: 239–257.

Soderberg, P. 2003. An examination of problem-based teaching and learning in population genetics and evolution using EVOLVE, a computer simulation. *International Journal of Science Education 25* (1): 35–55.

Songer, N. B. 1996. Exploring learning opportunities in coordinated network-enhanced classrooms: A case of kids as global scientists. *Journal of Learning Sciences* 5: 297–327.

Songer, N. B. 1998. Can technology bring students closer to science? In *The international handbook of science education,* eds. B. J. Frasier, and K. G. Tobin, 333–348. Dordrecht, The Netherlands: Kluwer Academic.

Songer, N. B., H. Lee, and R. Kam. 2002. Technology-rich inquiry science in urban classrooms: What are the barriers to inquiry pedagogy? *Journal of Research in Science Teaching*, 39(2): 128–150.

Sybol, T., and S. A. Southerland. 2005. *How does online assessment "fit" with the learning goals and discursive practices of an urban science classroom?* Paper presented at the annual meeting of the National Association for Research in Science Teaching, Dallas, TX.

Tal, R., and N. Hochberg. 2003. Assessing high order thinking of students participating in the "WISE" project in Israel. *Studies in Educational Evaluation* 29 (2): 69–89.

Tao, P., and R. Gunstone. 1999. The process of conceptual change in force and motion during computer-supported physics instruction. *Journal of Research in Science Teaching* 36 (7): 859–882.

TERC. 1986. *KIDNET*. A proposal submitted to the National Science Foundation. Cambridge, MA: Author.

Tinker, R. 2004. *A history of probeware*. Available online from the Stanford University website at *http://makingsens.stanford.edu/pubs/AHistoryOfProbeware.pdf*

Trundle, K., and R. Bell. 2005. *The use of a computer simulation to promote scientific conceptions of moon phases*. Paper presented at the NARST 2005 annual meeting, Dallas, TX.

U.S. Department of Labor. 2006. *The president's high growth job training initiative.* Available online at *www.doleta.gov/BRG/JobTrainInitiative*

Walberg, H. J., R. A. Paschal, and T. Weinstein. 1985. Homework's powerful effects on learning. *Educational Leadership* 42 (7): 76–79.

Wallace A.R. 1855. On the law which has regulated the introduction of new species. *Annals and Magazine of Natural History* 26: 184–196.

Web-Based Education Commission. 2000. The power of the internet for learning: Moving from promise to practice. Available online from the U.S. Department of Education website: *www.ed.gov/offices/AC/WBEC/FinalReport/WBECReport.pdf*

Weidenmann, B. 1989. When good pictures fail: An information-processing approach to the effect of illustrations. In *Knowledge acquisition from text and pic-*

tures, eds. H. Mandl, and J. R. Levin, 157–170. Amsterdam: Elsevier Science.

Wigglesworth, J. 2000. *Spatial problem-solving strategies of middle school students: Wayfinding with geographic information systems*. Unpublished doctoral dissertation. Boston University.

Windschitl, M. 1998. Independent student inquiry: Unlocking the resources of the World Wide Web. *NASSP Bulletin* 82: 93–98.

Wolpert, L. 1992. *The unnatural nature of science. Why science does not make (common) sense?* Cambridge, MA: Harvard University Press.

About the Authors

Thomas R. Baker is assistant research professor at the Center for Science Education, University of Kansas in Lawrence, Kansas.

Lynn Bell works at the Center for Technology and Teacher Education, University of Virginia in Charlottesville, Virginia and serves as managing editor of the online journal Contemporary Issues in Technology and Teacher Education (www.CITE-Journal.org).

Randy L. Bell is associate professor at the Curry School of Education, University of Virginia in Charlottesville, Virginia.

Alec M. Bodzin is associate professor in the Teaching, Learning, and Technology/ Department of Education and Human Services, Lehigh University in Bethlehem, Pennsylvania.

Glen Bull is professor of instructional technology in the Curry School of Education at the University of Virginia in Charlottesville, Virginia.

Tom Dana is professor and director of the School of Teaching and Learning, College of Education at University of Florida in Gainesville, Florida.

Rick Ferdig is associate professor at the School of Teaching and Learning, College of Education at University of Florida in Gainesville, Florida.

Julie Gess-Newsome is the J. Lawrence Walkup Distinguished Professor of Science Education, Department of Teaching and Learning at Northern Arizona University in Flagstaff, Arizona.

Taryn L. S. Hess is a PhD candidate and graduate research assistant at the College of Education, Educational Research, Technology, and Leadership Department, University of Central Florida in Orlando, Florida.

Julie Luft is professor of science education at Mary Lou Felton College of Education in Tempe, Arizona.

John C. Park is associate professor in the Department of Mathematics, Science, and Technology Education at North Carolina State University in Raleigh, North Carolina.

Lara K. Smetana is a doctoral student at the Curry School of Education, University of Virginia in Charlottesville, Virginia.

Sherry A. Southerland is associate professor of science education at the School of Teacher Education, Florida State University in Tallahassee, Florida.

Kathy Cabe Trundle is assistant professor of science education in the School of Teaching and Learning, The Ohio State University in Columbus, Ohio.

Index

F

G

H

I

U

V

W